Reading
Marechera

Published Works
by Dambudzo Marechera

The House of Hunger (1978)
Black Sunlight (1980)
Mindblast, or, The Definitive Buddy (1984)
The Black Insider (1992)
Cemetery of Mind (1992)
Scrapiron Blues (1994)

Reading Marechera

edited by
GRANT HAMILTON
Assistant Professor of English Literature
at the Chinese University of Hong Kong

JAMES CURREY

James Currey
is an imprint of Boydell & Brewer Ltd
PO Box 9, Woodbridge,
Suffolk IP12 3DF (GB)
www.jamescurrey.com

and of

Boydell & Brewer Inc.
668 Mt Hope Avenue
Rochester, NY 14620-2731 (US)
www.boydellandbrewer.com

Distributed in Zimbabwe by
Weaver Press
PO Box A1922, Avondale
Harare
Zimbabwe
www.weaverpresszimbabwe.com

Every effort has been made to trace the copyright holder
of the photograph on the cover and on p. xiii.

British Library Cataloguing in Publication Data
A catalogue record for this book is available
on request from the British Library

ISBN 978-1-84701-062-9 James Currey (Paper)

The publisher has no responsibility for the continued existence or accuracy of URLs for external
or third-party internet websites referred to in this book, and does not guarantee that any content
on such websites is, or will remain, accurate or appropriate.

Papers used by Boydell & Brewer are natural, recycled products
made from wood grown in sustainable forests.

Designed and typeset in 12.5/15 Berkeley Old Style
by Kate Kirkwood, Long House Publishing Services
Printed and bound in the United
States of America

Contents

Notes on Contributors

Bill Ashcroft
Professor of English Literature at the University of New South Wales, Australia. A renowned critic and theorist, Bill Ashcroft is a founding exponent of post-colonial theory and co-author of the first text to examine systematically the field of post-colonial studies, *The Empire Writes Back* (Routledge, 1989). In addition to this, he has written or co-authored sixteen books and over 150 scholarly articles and book chapters. His most recent books are *Post-Colonial Transformation* (Routledge, 2001), *On Post-Colonial Futures* (Continuum, 2001), and *Caliban's Voice* (Routledge, 2009).

Memory Chirere
A prize-winning Zimbabwean writer, Memory Chirere enjoys reading and writing short stories, some of which are published in *No More Plastic Balls* (College Press, 1999), *A Roof to Repair* (College Press, 2000), *Writing Still* (Weaver Press, 2003), and *Creatures Great and Small* (Mambo Press, 2005). He has also published three short story books: *Somewhere in this Country* (UNISA Press, 2006), *Tudikidiki* (Priority, 2007) and *Toriro and His Goats* (Lion Press, 2010). Together with Professor Maurice Vambe, he has compiled and edited *Charles Mungoshi: A Critical Reader* (Prestige Books, 2006). He lectures in literature at the University of Zimbabwe.

Grant Hamilton
Assistant professor with the Department of English, Chinese University of Hong Kong. He has published in the fields of

African literature, post-colonial literature and theory, and the philosophy of Gilles Deleuze. His most recent work is *On Representation: Deleuze and Coetzee on the Colonized Subject* (Rodopi, 2011).

David Huddart
Associate professor of English Literature at the Chinese University of Hong Kong. He is the author of *Homi K. Bhabha* (Routledge, 2005) and *Postcolonial Theory and Autobiography* (Routledge, 2008). He researches post-colonial theory, literature, and world Englishes.

Madhlozi Moyo
Lecturer in Classics at the University of Zimbabwe. His areas of teaching include Greek and Latin languages as well as Classical literature, art, and archaeology. His most recent scholarly work discusses the use of animal tales in Apuleius and the African novel. In addition to this, he is also a published novelist and poet. His most recent poetry appears in the collection *Ghetto Diary and Other Poems* (Zimbabwe Publishing House, 2011).

Tinashe Mushakavanhu
Recently completed a PhD in English at the University of Kent where he also works as an assistant lecturer in English. He also holds degrees from universities in Wales and Zimbabwe and is co-editor of *State of the Nation: Contemporary Zimbabwean Poetry* (The Conversation Paperpress, 2009) and *Visa Stories: Experiences Between Law and Migration* (Cambridge Scholars Publishing, 2012). He is currently working on a critical volume on the writings of Chenjerai Hove.

Anias Mutekwa
Graduated from the University of Zimbabwe in 2002 and has been a lecturer in the department of English and Communication, Midlands State University, Gweru, Zimbabwe since

2004. His main interests are in the areas of African literature, gender studies, literature and environment, spirit possession in literature, and second language pedagogy.

Eddie Tay
Assistant professor with the Department of English, Chinese University of Hong Kong. His research interests are in the areas of creative writing (poetry) as well as colonial and post-colonial literature – especially Singaporean and Malaysian literatures written in English. His most recent scholarly work is titled *Colony, Nation, and Globalization: Not at Home in Singaporean and Malaysian Literature* (Hong Kong University Press, 2011; NUS Press, 2011). His third poetry collection is titled *The Mental Life of Cities* (Chameleon Press, 2010).

Anna-Leena Toivanen
Currently working as a postdoctoral researcher at the University of Eastern Finland. Her recent publications include, '"At the Receiving End of Severe Misunderstanding": Representations of Authorship in Dambudzo Marechera's Work,' *Research in African Literatures* 42.1 (2011); 'Celles qui attendent et l'engagement diasporique de Fatou Diome' Revue *RELIEF* 5.1 (2011); and, 'Writing Bodies: Yvonne Vera's Insights into Empowering Female Corporeality' in *Emerging Perspectives on Yvonne Vera*. eds Helen Cousins and Pauline Dodgson-Katiyo (Africa World Press, 2012). In her ongoing research project, she is interested in critically revising some claims of the postnationalist paradigm by focusing on the tensions of nationhood and globalization in Sub-Saharan African women's writing.

Mark P. Williams
Originally from the UK, Mark P. Williams is a journalist and independent researcher currently residing in Wellington, New Zealand. He gained his PhD in English Literature from

the University of East Anglia. His recent work includes a chapter on British small press writing and decadent aesthetics in the anthology *Gothic Science Fiction 1980-2010* (Liverpool UP, 2011) and forthcoming chapters in the UK Network for Modern Fiction Studies *Decades* anthologies: a literary history for *The 1970s: A Decade of Contemporary Fiction*, and a study of experimental fiction for *The 1990s: A Decade of Contemporary Fiction*. He is presently a political reporter for Scoop Media (http://www.scoop.co.nz), where he co-edits the *Scoop Review of Books*, and writes articles on politics in contemporary literature and culture for *Werewolf* (http://www.werewolf.co.nz), edited by Gordon Campbell.

Dambudzo Marechera in his Harare flat, 1984/5
(With thanks to Flora Veit-Wild; photographer unknown)

Introduction
Marechera & the Outside

GRANT HAMILTON

In perhaps his most widely read essay, 'The African Writer's Experience of European Literature,' Dambudzo Marechera introduces himself as a person who is 'inclined to disagree with everybody and everything.'[1] It is at once a light-hearted and deeply provocative self-characterization. Undoubtedly, Marechera did not mind being regarded as the *enfant terrible* of African literature. Indeed, much of what he said and did painted him in this particular way. His exploits off the page married with the visceral ideas and images that he committed to it, created the myth of the man which would always precede him. So, as he returned to Zimbabwe from his exile in Europe:

> Press coverage recounted the highlights of his legendary career: the attempt to set fire to an Oxford college; throwing crockery at the *Guardian* Fiction Prize ceremony; the ban from his publishers' offices; detention and triumph in West Berlin.[2]

The image of Marechera was of an anarchic young contrarian, a maverick, a rebel who stood against everything simply because he could. And, this is certainly the impression we are left with when we learn that Marechera spoke against Ian Smith's minority regime, declaring himself a supporter of Robert Mugabe, only to then declare his opposition to Mugabe when he later took the reins of government.[3]

---

[1] Dambudzo Marechera, 'The African Writer's Experience of European Literature,' *Zambezia* 14, no. 2 (1987), 99.

[2] Flora Veit-Wild, *Dambudzo Marechera: A Source Book on his Life and Work* (London: Hans Zell, 1992), 282.

[3] See Helon Habila, 'On Dambudzo Marechera: The Life and Times of an African Writer,' *The Virginian Quarterly Review* (Winter, 2006), 251-60.

1

But, what at first we might think of as the simple adoption and rendition of oppositionality becomes something significantly different when we recognize the quality and energy of the thought that lies behind such antagonistic pronouncements. For Marechera, it is not necessarily for their politics that Smith, Mugabe, and all the other 'leaders' of the world should be challenged. What is to be challenged is the way in which these people assume the ability to control the lives of innumerable others. Making his point clear in an interview with Alle Lansu, Marechera says, 'the very thought that someone has got enough power to organize thousands of people's lives, whether he makes a mistake or not, really horrifies me.'[4] Here, then, is a glimpse of the thought that underlines Marechera's confrontational stance. At this moment we realize that his oppositionality to Ian Smith and Robert Mugabe is not unthinkingly reactionary but rather arises from the point of a pure ethics – that all people should be equal. Nothing can be more ethically sound than this.

It is, then, the way in which life seems to endlessly deviate from this simple egalitarian desire that forms the material of Marechera's combative writing. And, the notions of leaders and leadership are often his focus. Indeed, leaders are a very good example of the way in which life seems to impose an imbalance in the relationship between people. For Marechera, the very structure of leadership is an affront to his simple, yet profoundly revolutionary, sense of ethics. Leadership inhibits individual thought and practices, privileging instead adherence to exclusive structures of belonging such as ideology and traditionalism. All of this is to be excised. Marechera's revolutionary ethics damns exclusionary epistemological and ontological models. Indeed, he refuses to play the game of identification and exclusion demanded by the Manichean models so often employed by sitting governments and, perhaps more worryingly, cultures. At his dismissive best, Marechera writes:

---

[4] Alle Lansu, 'Escape from the "House of Hunger:" Marechera Talks about His Life,' in *Dambudzo Marechera: A Source Book on his Life and Work*, 33.

I do not like this century. I do not like any other century, past or future. I do not like to live under the backside of a medieval god or a nuclear bomb, which amounts to the same thing. I am no mystic, yet no materialist either. I believe in nature but refuse to live with it in the same room.[5]

This is the articulation of a man who refuses to be positioned so that he can be called upon by others to write against his beliefs. It is the articulation of a man who recognizes that perhaps the only position that he can comfortably inhabit is that of the eccentric – literally the ex-centric, the outsider. Unlike those on the fringes of political discourse, those who appeal to ever more specific and seemingly arcane political causes, Marechera thinks of himself as 'the outsider.' He reflects, 'I have been an outsider in my own biography, in my country's history.'[6] For Marechera, to be an outsider is the only way to truly free oneself from what *must* be said, or what *ought* to be said, in order to think of what *can* be said – what French philosopher Gilles Deleuze rightly calls an ethics without morality.[7] Without the binds of consenting to a particular ideology, form or function of traditionalism, history, morality, or even the self, Marechera casts himself as a truly original, and therefore revolutionary, thinker.

This space of the outside, the space of the original thinker, is a location that is also shared from time-to-time with the thoughts of the exile. It is a space that Marechera knew well, given that he too was also exiled from Zimbabwe. Contemplating his own exilic condition, he reflects:

It takes only an instant to become a person without titles, without a label, to become the raw person, the point at which low-life naturalism meets its *doppelgänger*, the existentialist.[8]

[5] Marechera, 'The African Writer's Experience,' 101.
[6] Ibid., 102.
[7] Gilles Deleuze, *Negotiations, 1972-1990*, trans. Martin Joughin (New York: Columbia UP, 1995), 100.
[8] Marechera, 'The African Writer's Experience,' 104.

For Edward Said, the experience of being forcibly denuded of social and filial relationships makes exile a terrible form of 'mutilation.'[9] Marechera, I think, would agree with this assertion. However, in this mutilated, raw state where the only element of consequence left is the self, Marechera finds the basest and thereby the most profound revelations of mind. After all, it is here that one experiences the marriage of low-life naturalism and existentialism. Writing produced by this union, Marechera's writing, is a raw and vital literature. Stripped of the gift of pretence or homage to the celebrated name, Marechera's writing is more than the mere reiteration of his life; it is the writing of life. Deleuze saw this quality in all great writers. He explains:

> You don't write with your ego, your memory, and your illnesses. In the act of writing there's an attempt to make life something more than personal, to free life from what imprisons it.[10]

Many have mistakenly thought that Marechera did exactly this – write with his ego, memory, or madness. But, of course, quite the reverse is true. Marechera's writing taps into the vitalism of life and in so doing enters into a realm of universality and essentialism that positions it as a non-personal *singular* rather than *specific* expression of the world. Deleuze offers an interesting way to think of the distinction between the singular and the specific. According to Deleuze, the singular is best understood through the indeterminate infinitive form of the verb – to be; to laugh; to run. Before this verb form is actualized, that is to say before it is determined through specific 'modes, tenses, persons, and voices'[11] – *I am*; *he* laugh*ed*; *we will* run – it engenders the innumerable possibilities of life. So, as

---

[9] Edward Said, 'The Mind of Winter: Reflections on Life in Exile,' *Harper's Magazine*, September, 1984, 50.

[10] Gilles Deleuze, *Negotiations*, 143.

[11] Daniel W. Smith, Introduction to *Essays Critical and Clinical*, by Gilles Deleuze, trans. Daniel W. Smith and Michael Greco (London: Verso, 1998), xxv.

Daniel Smith notes, 'such singularities constitute the genetic elements not only of an individual life, but also of the world in which they are actualized.'[12] Marechera may have fictionalized elements of his own life in his writing, but he did so only to test a philosophical universalism that could contemplate the world on the broadest possible scale. It is this that Marechera understands when he writes, 'eternity contained within the finite, the permanent within the temporal. We are provisional yet have the seeds of limitlessness.'[13] Zimbabwean writer George Kahari frames Marechera's appeal to the singular like this: 'Marechera's message is not only appealing to the moral sentiment of his own people, but the sentiment of all mankind – the universal man.'[14]

So, Marechera's non-linear, discontinuous, fractured narratives are a means of trying to free 'life' from what imprisons it. Without the restrictions and limitations of expression announced by the preachers of literature, the fantastic, vital current of life that lies just beneath the surface of the world presents itself. One current that Marechera recognizes as a particularly powerful conditioning force of contemporary society is that of World War II. It was an event that was so powerful that, as Albert Camus saw, it did not only turn the world upside down; it reoriented morality by putting the innocence of the post-war generation on trial.[15] As a consequence of an age that has put innocence on trial, Marechera states that 'we have become ruthless enough to judge while cynically knowing that judgment is useless, beside the point. The judge and the accused know that both of them are guilty and the trial a farce.'[16] We may take part in this pretense of society, but each of us understands that the apparatuses by which we are told to know, understand, and live in the world are empty of any

---

[12] Ibid., xxv.
[13] Marechera, 'The African Writer's Experience,' 102.
[14] George Kahari, *The Search for Identity and Ufuru* (Gweru: Mambo Press, 2009), 189.
[15] Albert Camus, *The Rebel*, trans. Anthony Bower (1951; London: Penguin, 2000), 12.
[16] Marechera, 'The African Writer's Experience,' 102.

significance. In the knowledge of the moral and ethical vacuity of social systems, we can only stand on the outside of what Louis Althusser calls the Ideological State Apparatuses,[17] or, as Marechera suggests, 'flee from the excesses of our parents.'[18]

For Marechera, the post-war generation is then, in this very specific way, a generation of exiles. Fleeing the horrors perpetrated on the earth, and the minds and bodies of others by the hand of our parents, the demand is made on the writer to first make known the need to craft a better, more ethical world and, secondly, to consider the conditions whereby the unfettered imagination can be actualized on the earth. It is this program that both renders the dissident writer and unites him with others – Jan Pelc, Wole Soyinka, Albert Camus, Jack Kerouac, Andrei Sinyavsky, John Kennedy Toole. In their own ways, each of these writers is a visionary who either rails against the vacuity of contemporary society or tries to apprehend the vital, fantastic world that lies just beneath the surface of 'the real.' It is this that makes them truly revolutionary writers; but it is also this that will see them always-already cast into opposition to a state that will treat them as a cancer to be excised.

In order to show both the absence at the core of contemporary society and intimate the essential singular force that powers 'the real,' Marechera embarks on perhaps the most profound kind of exile – exile from the self. Reflecting on the act of critiquing the literary imagination, he writes:

> If I am looking at something, and I am conscious of myself looking, does that affect what I see? Can I learn to experience the world from that quality in us which is the source of dreams?[19]

---

[17] Louis Althusser, 'Ideology and Ideological State Apparatuses,' in *Lenin and Philosophy and Other Essays*, trans. Ben Brewster (London: Monthly Review Press, 1971), 127-88.

[18] Marechera, 'The African Writer's Experience,' 102.

[19] Ibid., 99.

This is a strong indication that Marechera has the ability to think of himself as an 'other.' In the creation of this other self – 'the inquisitor' as he later comes to term it – Marechera seems to complete his search for the absolute outside. In this moment when he observes himself regarding something else, Marechera is not merely outside of politics, ideology, literary history, morality, and so on, he is outside of himself. Here, the young contrarian confronts the rebel and the last vestige of deceit and conceit falls away so that the world can be seen as a unique, profound, singular force.

But, if we were to think that the space of the 'absolute outside' was also the space of Marechera's 'absolute solitude' we would be wrong. It is in this space that Marechera finds a universe of thought that promises the only kind of respite from his condition of exile that he is willing to accept. Here, the writing of Marechera sits alongside the writing of other intellectual outsiders – Jorge Louis Borges, Giovanni Boccaccio, Guy de Maupassant, Petronius, Novalis, Percy Bysshe Shelley, Amos Tutuola, Friedrich Hölderlin, Allen Ginsberg, Frantz Fanon, Mikhail Bakhtin, Anthony Burgess, Jean Genet, James Joyce, Günter Grass, Apuleius, Alexander Pushkin, Fyodor Dostoyevsky. It is this universe of literary thought that one can see written into the fiction of Marechera that this collection of essays sets out to interrogate. It is a way in which we can begin to understand the quality of Marechera's own writing, as it enters into this universe and in turn inspires writers yet-to-come.

The collection begins with the connections that Tinashe Mushakavanhu draws between the life and work of Percy Bysshe Shelley and Dambudzo Marechera. Mushakavanhu argues that Shelley and Marechera share more than simply an anarchic sense of humor that sees them both try to burn down an Oxford college! Indeed, both writers seem to share a fundamental appreciation of what happens when the mind cracks open to expose its otherwise subconscious content.

In their episodes of 'madness,' both writers reveal a political mind that has the capacity to see into the most vital structures and energies of society. From this arises their shared project – to write the subterranean socio-political forces into common understanding.

Anias Mutekwa's essay fleshes out the significance of anarchist thought to Marechera's writing. Considering the difference in nineteenth-century and late-twentieth-century visions of anarchism, Mutekwa positions Marechera as an 'intellectual anarchist' of the avant-garde. In this way, he is a 'monster of the intellectual order.' Marechera, it seems, is feared by those who wish to promote a particular spirit of intellectual or cultural life, and celebrated by those who appreciate the liberatory force of his vision of radical individualism.

In Marechera's best known essay, he laments the quiescence that describes African literature's examination of the psychology or anatomy of violence.[20] Of course, Marechera is known for the violent images that he lets loose on the page. It is, then, in the interest of trying to understand the significance of violence in Marechera's writing that Anna-Leena Toivanen turns towards Marechera's novella 'House of Hunger.' Drawing from the ideas of Mikhail Bakhtin that so readily appealed to Marechera, Toivanen thinks of the Marecheran grotesque as a form of resistance to both the colonial order and its anti-colonial, nationalist sequel.

My contribution to this collection also centers on Marechera's 'House of Hunger.' Partly as a means of defending Marechera's writing from the critics with a vested interest in a very particular literary aesthetic, partly as a means of simply revealing some of the complexity of Marechera's political thought, my essay interrogates the significance of Marechera's *ritournelle* of 'the stain.' I argue that the ubiquitous stain is the material fact of the Derridean 'trace.' As such, it merely highlights the condition of 'absent presence' that Marechera finds in the 'new' – but not 'revolutionary' – independent state of Zimbabwe.

[20] Ibid., 100.

Bill Ashcroft's paper examines the difficult stylistics at play in Marechera's writing. After reading the incredibly rich work of Mikhail Bakhtin, Marechera powerfully concludes that, 'it is no longer necessary to speak of the African novel or the European novel: there is only the menippean novel.'[21] For Marechera, the 'African novel' or the 'European novel' are unhelpful forms of limitation. Indeed, they are poor descriptors employed by unthinking people who own an impoverished understanding of the complex dynamic in which all literature takes part. Only the menippean novel, with its acceptance of the limitless possibilities of writing, is durable enough to describe literature. It is, then, the idea and the mechanics of the menippean novel as employed by Marechera that Ashcroft confronts.

It is the way in which the menippean novel antagonizes and ultimately collapses borders of thought and expression that leads David Huddart to question the autobiographical nature of Marechera's writing. Seeing clear parallels between Marechera's constant return to his own life and the way in which important Martiniquan thinker Frantz Fanon rendered his own revolutionary psychopathology of colonization, Huddart turns to *The Black Insider* to show the stress that both writers place on the infinite possibility of the future.

For both Marechera and Frantz Fanon, part of the allure of the future is that it has the capacity to crystallize unforeseen, forgotten, perhaps latent forces of the present. Staging just this process, Mark Williams comments on the significance of Marechera's lauded novel *Black Sunlight* to two provocative contemporary writers – British Marxist fantasy novelist China Miéville and American performance artist and writer Darius James. Williams sees Marechera, Miéville, and James as part of an internationalist avant-garde with the ability to write across differentiation, assimilation, genre, and cultural traditions. Together, such writers might form an 'anti-canon;' but it is the way in which the work of these writers simultaneously takes

[21] Ibid., 101.

part in, sustains, yet also challenges the powerful discursive forms resident within globalization that interests Williams.

After considering the influence of Marechera's work on the contemporary, global circuit of world writing, Madhlozi Moyo asks us to consider the meaning of Marechera's often-noted recourse to the writing from the ancient Mediterranean world. Moyo argues that it is with the continued use of classical allusion that we can see the particular kind of universalism – essentialism even – that appeals to Marechera. For Marechera, Western literary antiquity has a wisdom to which the contemporary world still remains deaf.

Memory Chirere's paper highlights the importance of a particular play in Flora Veit-Wild's posthumous collection of Marechera's writing, *Scrapiron Blues*. As Chirere makes clear, the play 'The Servants' Ball' is the only example we have of Marechera's writing in Shona. Since Marechera demonstrates much skill in his use of Shona in this play, the question we are quickly drawn to consider is why Marechera seemingly stopped writing in this language in favor of English. As such, 'The Servants' Ball' reignites the explosive debate over the place of the English language in African literary expression. It is Marechera's position in this debate that Chirere considers.

The collection ends with Eddie Tay's beautiful reflection on Marechera's poetry. A poet reading a poet, Tay suggests that although the cleverness of Marechera's writing might invite critical analysis – the dogged interrogation of his writing that goes along with projects such as this one – we should rather leave it alone. We should let it breathe, unused, unproductive, unclaimed, in order that we preserve the possibilities of his poetry that we have yet to learn to read.

There are, then, many ways to read Marechera, some of them yet to be discovered. And so this collection of essays on Marechera's writing can do nothing other than present itself as a tentative step into the territory of Marechera's literary universe.

1

A Brotherhood of Misfits
The Literary Anarchism of Dambudzo Marechera & Percy Bysshe Shelley

TINASHE MUSHAKAVANHU

I first encountered Dambudzo Marechera at an out of way boarding school in the farming district of Selous in Mashonaland west province in Zimbabwe. I was 14 years old. Our small school library had a full collection of all Marechera books. *The House of Hunger* was the first book I read. I vividly remember moments I would sit under library tables or hide behind colossal bookshelves and read a Marechera book. Reading Marechera was like an initiation into a secret society. There was something wonderfully subversive about his writing; he said things that were too dangerous to say, things that we all knew but couldn't say. In this way, Marechera prompted me to pursue him.

I saw in his fictional creations the streets in which my mother and father grew up, the streets in which I was growing up – the hunger, the squalor, the poverty, the prostitution. Literature became the motion picture of my existence. And then something happened. In 2006 I made my first trip to Europe, and in my travelling bag I carried with me the Marechera books I owned – a blurry photocopy of *The House of Hunger* with missing pages, and *The Black Insider*. Interestingly, of these books, it would prove to be *The Black Insider* that would have the most profound effect on me.

I spent a year as the only black student on campus. And suddenly, *The Black Insider*, made sense – the identity issues, the problem of race, exile, nationalism. Though inadvertently, I was following in Marechera's footsteps. Fortunately, I didn't end up in a Cardiff jail like he did. I was a student of Creative Writing at Trinity College, Carmarthen where I became the first African to receive the degree. The experience was isolating at times, never getting to see people of my color, never getting to laugh and speak in my own language. There is always baggage that comes with that, this feeling that you are constantly on display, being judged and stereotyped and never knowing quite how people feel about you. I started hanging out with Marechera and his characters. His books became companions. And, then one day I was introduced to a young Romantic poet, Percy Bysshe Shelley, who had just been expelled from University College, Oxford. I became so fascinated with his story.

During this time, I worked in the college library and instead of stacking shelves, spent most of the time squatting on the carpets reading everything I could find on Shelley and the Romantics. The story I was reading echoed what I already knew of Marechera's story. I decided then to go and study at Oxford and rather than get expelled like Marechera and Shelley, maybe try to understand the institution and why they couldn't fit. This matched a dream my parents had for me. From the age of ten, they were on about Cambridge or Oxford. But after correspondences with a prominent professor about a thesis on Marechera and Shelley I was left discouraged. She thought it was a 'crazy pairing' and besides, she continued, 'I'm not sure how Oxford would be positioned *vis-à-vis* a project that drew on the writer's own creative writing practices...' I took my things and left. For Zimbabwe. But, I returned. This time to the small city that Chaucer had immortalized – Canterbury. Here, in Canterbury, I have been working on this 'crazy pairing' of Marechera and Shelley.

A major characteristic ubiquitous within Marechera and Shelley is a defiant overcoming of the limits set by historically imposed structures that would limit their range of expression, their engagement with politics, and the nature of social interaction. What is clear is their intellectual fluidity; their vast references to literary allusions and philosophies, perhaps suggesting that the human mind is a multiplicity of selves. To understand those selves, is to understand others, and society as a whole. In fact, this is the key to the philosophy that pervades their works and attitudes.

From very young ages, Marechera and Shelley defied rules and limits. They always created holes through the fence of tradition to go and experience what was on the other side. They went beyond set boundaries in order to spread the seeds of their ideas and undermine what Rolando Perez calls 'the repressive coding of institutions.'[1] Both rely on their imagination to question constantly naturalized values.

What is particularly interesting about Marechera and Shelley is that they are at the height of their powers very early in their writing careers, as young men on the threshold of adulthood. Even though both are expelled from the University of Oxford and denied academic honors, it seems they both graduate from the institution as writers. They begin to define the world around them and be defined by their writings. And what sets them apart from their peers is that they are always willing to walk the tightrope. For this one must have courage, because to live as a human being independent of the morality of traditions and systems and institutions is not easy. The refusals to conform to external expectations had their corollary in both Marechera's and Shelley's attempts to map the psychological forms of freedom and mental imprisonment in their works. They take us to a deeper level of questioning and thinking about power, corruption, values and even identities. Their abilities, still celebrated today, are not just to scrutinize their everyday problems but to diagnose the underlying psychological problems. *The House of Hunger* and all the subsequent Marechera books give an inward gaze into the workings of the mind and the complex situational and circumstantial factors that affect it. And the Shelley catalogue of poetry is suffused with inspired moral optimism, which he hoped would affect his readers sensuously, spiritually, and morally.

Marechera's and Shelley's lives and writings provide the

[1] Rolando Perez, *An(archy) and Schizoanalysis* (New York: Automedia, 1990), 17.

blueprint for a psychology of anarchism. They had unstable childhoods, uneasy relationships with parents, and it is their reaction to the family that makes them question and appreciate the psychologically undergirding structures of social and political power. The social functioning of the family as David Cooper describes is as 'an ideological conditioning device,'[2] the ultimate factor that leads individuals to accept the circumstances they find themselves in, however dehumanizing. In fact, the power of the family resides in its social mediating function. It reinforces the effective power of the ruling class in any exploitative society by providing a highly controllable paradigmatic form for every social institution. Both writers notice from a very young age that the family form is replicated through the social structures of the school, the university, the church, political parties, the governmental apparatus, the armed forces, even hospitals and so on. That is to say, that the family is firmly embedded in what Louis Althusser calls the Ideological State Apparatuses.

This structuralization and desire of control is clearly what Marechera and Shelley were against. Like a streetcar named 'Desire,' whose direction is controlled by the lines which run beneath it, the restrictiveness of the Oedipal structure often results in stunted growth. The first act of liberation that Marechera and Shelley do is dismantle their family structures, because, as Perez rightly points out, 'how close one remains to mommy and daddy or how far one strays from them determines the degrees of someone's sense of guilt.'[3] The family usually turns the child's body into a docile body. This is why the breaking of rules, the going beyond of traditional (family) morality is so very difficult and yet so necessary. One must somehow be able to see through the rules and all the restrictions behind them. And then to make matters even more difficult, one must be willing to take a chance with one's so called 'sanity' in order to break the rules. Put simply, one must

---

[2] David Cooper, *The Death of the Family* (Middlesex: Penguin Books, 1971), 5.
[3] Perez, *An(archy) and Schizoanalysis*, 24.

be 'mad' to question or rebuke what everyone else perceives to be normal. Until his death, Marechera was considered to be mad, *mupengo*, and Shelley was even known as 'mad Shelley.' However, it seems that in order to be as radical and forthright as they were one needed to be eccentric – literally outside of the center.

Marechera and Shelley are two of a kind in terms of anticipating the notion that revolutionary change can come out of a descent into the terrain of psychological immanence. Extreme experiences of psychological violence whilst growing up turn them towards anarchism. Both suffer nervous breakdowns – many of the testimonies of Marechera's friends recorded by Flora Veit-Wild recount stories of his psychological illness.[4] Much like the narrator's account in Marechera's 'House of Hunger,' Shelley also suffered from hallucinations, commenting that he had witnessed the movement of shadowy figures whilst at boarding school. Hence, both writers seem to have a more fundamental appreciation of what happens when the mind cracks open to reveal its otherwise subconscious content. Their appreciation is deeper in that it takes us towards possibilities of a complete fluidity and regeneration, an overhaul of the self, inside out. This, then, is the terrain of the writing of Shelley and Marechera. Such difficult psychological episodes break the pattern of social and cultural inevitabilities, and allow the writers to think beyond the ordinary. In this way, Marechera and Shelley can be thought of as 'wake up writers.' That was their revolutionary mission, as I see it, both on and off the page. Theirs was a mission to 'shock' readers with the scandalous detail of everyday existence. So, Marechera renders the dark side of Rhodesian society, a system of institutionalized patronage and state-sponsored violence in *The House of Hunger*. Similarly, Shelley's *Queen Mab* is read as a fantastical tale of revolution and emancipation that is pirated and eventually

---

[4] Flora Veit-Wild, *Dambudzo Marechera: A Source Book on his Life and Work* (London: Hans Zell, 1992).

adopted as a bible for the laboring classes. In each instance, these confrontational writers seem to wake people from the slumber of their historically limiting circumstances.

Shelley's work is marked by a poetic commitment to social amelioration in the Godwinian sense. Indeed, Peter Marshall describes Shelley as 'the greatest anarchist poet,' he who effectively put 'William Godwin's philosophy to verse.'[5] Godwin's philosophy was articulated in his influential book, *Political Justice*, published in 1793.[6] Here Godwin envisaged a utopian society governed entirely by reason. Shelley systematically celebrated the Godwinian principles of liberty, equality and universal benevolence that prepared for a utopia he envisioned in his epic poems such as *Queen Mab* and *Prometheus Unbound*. Marechera, though, is different. He, like Mikhail Bakunin, the classical anarchist thinker whom he read and confessed an admiration for in an interview with the Dutch journalist Alle Lansu,[7] celebrates destruction and chaos in his writings, which may be because he felt it was first necessary to destroy 'the old' in order to create 'the new.' But, in destroying, Marechera is not preparing to build, rather simply to provoke. This is perhaps the clearest way to think of his use of language and the vivid imagery he employs in his prose and poetry. Marechera, unlike Shelley, seems to have adopted anarchism as a mental tool to deal with his sense of futility in everything conditioned by a childhood in an oppressive colonial environment. In his world nothing is allowed to succeed and the only constant and exception to this rule is change itself. He says:

> anarchism is full of contradictions in the sense that it can never achieve its goals. If it achieves any goal at all, then it is no longer anarchism. And so one has to be in a perpetual state of change,

[5] Peter Marshall, *Demanding the Impossible: A History of Anarchism* (London: Fontana, 1993), 192.

[6] William Godwin, *Enquiry Concerning Political Justice: with selections from Godwin's other writings* (Oxford: Clarendon Publishers, 1971).

[7] Alle Lansu, 'Escape from the "House of Hunger:" Marechera Talks about His Life,' in *Dambudzo Marechera: A Source Book on his Life and Work*, 1-48.

without holding on to any certainties. And that element I put across seriously as well as in a very frivolous vein.[8]

While Marechera is nihilistic and skeptical of power and politics, Shelley is optimistic for the reforming potential of poetry. What is fascinating about both, though, is that they respond with righteous anger and keen political intent to acts of extreme brutality by ruling powers. In 'The Masque of Anarchy,' a poem Shelley writes in response to the St Peterloo massacre of 1819 in which fifteen people were killed and hundreds injured after a court-sanctioned attack by the yeomanry, he writes:

> And many more Destructions played
> In this ghastly masquerade,
> All disguised, even to the eyes,
> Like Bishops, lawyers, peers or spies.[9]

Shelley's observation could as well be a litany of the many guises that the government in post-independence Zimbabwe would wear, and that is what is openly criticized in Marechera's works. Just as Shelley regards the various spheres of power in England in 1819 and the corruption beneath, so Marechera lampoons each sector of Zimbabwean governance with vicious precision. Shelley's task and Marechera's too is to ask the difficult questions and provoke a sense of moral outrage. As Marechera puts it:

> I try to write in such a way that I short-circuit, like in electricity, people's traditions and morals. Because only then can they start having original thoughts of their own. I would like people to stop thinking in an institutionalized way... that's why most of what I have written is always seen as being disruptive and destructive. For me, that slow brain death... can be cured by this kind of literary shock treatment.[10]

---

[8] Ibid., 31.
[9] Percy Bysshe Shelley, *The Masque of Anarchy* (London: Edward Moxon, 1832), 4.
[10] Veit-Wild, *Dambudzo Marechera*, 40-41.

Shelley's unequivocal rebelliousness against aristocratic social and political norms was mostly embodied in his passionate poetry, particularly the 1819 political poems that rebuke the powerful hegemonic triumvirate of God, Law and King, just as Marechera's radical struggle for decolonization in political and personal terms is effective in his fragmentary stories in *The House of Hunger*. In short, the existing social order in each case is seen as outrageously unjust. So, both Shelley and Marechera are rebellious and their writing acts like a literary shock therapy on the body-politic of their societies.

Hence both writers employ a similar iconography to grapple with the increasing violence deployed by the powerful minority on the powerless majority. This juxtaposition reveals how Marechera and Shelley attempt to challenge the status quo, and in so doing become unheralded representatives of the masses. In his polemical essay 'A Defence of Poetry,' Shelley describes poets, and by extension all writers, as 'unacknowledged legislators of the world'[11] since they often call into question the binary structures of the oppressor and oppressed. Indeed, both Marechera and Shelley are successful in their 'public roles' even though certain elements in their societies fundamentally disagree with them or try to rubbish their relevance. For example, Shelley's poem *Queen Mab* was pirated and circulated by the radical underground, including the Chartists, while 'The Masque of Anarchy' has been widely quoted in numerous occasions of political protest. Though it was published after Shelley's death, it came out at a time when there was heated debate about Parliamentary reforms in England. The poem also inspired the non-violent movement led by Mohandas K. Gandhi. The cult of Marechera is also growing. Young Zimbabweans in Harare and Johannesburg, for example, hold 'House of Hunger Poetry Slams' dedicated to Marechera. In Chielo Zona Eze's novel, *The Trial of Robert Mugabe* (2009), Marechera is a

---

[11] Percy Bysshe Shelley, *A Defence of Poetry and Other Essays* (Gloucester: Dodo Press, 2007), 70.

character among other literary figures like Yvonne Vera.[12] And, Rwandan actor, Ery Nzaramba, is currently making a biopic film on the life and times of Marechera. And so their enduring influence continues.

But during their times, Marechera and Shelley were perpetual exiles from their families, their traditions, their countries, and remained in a state of motion that is needed to lead an anarchical existence which is not bound by any form of loyalty or responsibility or social contract. The anarchist is a nomad – never one to remain dependent and static, always 'on the road' like Jack Kerouac. In moving you learn twice as much. Movement is important as it allows points of connections leading to what Deleuze and Guattari call 'a thousand of plateaus.'[13] Whether a writer ends up weaving more expansive versions of the possible into the limited political reality of his time, or exploding the reader's sense of everyday reality with new forms of radicalism, the creative interventions are designed to change the mentality of a people, into a kind of anarchic transcendence.

The year 1819 was a prolific year for Shelley. It sharpened his socio-political sensibilities, and his utmost skill was required to deal with events in his home country while resident in the distant Italy. The same can be said of Marechera in the 1970s as he looked back at events in Zimbabwe from London. If Shelley's 'The Masque of Anarchy' does not express a total loss of faith in politics, it at best shows faith sustained only by its mythologizing of political issues, making them rhetorical and symbolical 'properties' in a moral drama whose relation to the actual public case grows increasingly tenuous. Marechera's graphic account of society in the 'House of Hunger' is similarly powerful. He effectively condenses the anger of a colonized people and throws it back as a vitriolic bomb into the face

---

[12] Chielo Zona Eze, *The Trial of Robert Mugabe* (Chicago: Okri Books, 2009).
[13] Gilles Deleuze and Félix Guattari, *A Thousand Plateaus: Capitalism and Schizophrenia 2*, trans. Brian Massumi (London: Athlone, 1988).

of Empire. He undresses power politics and unashamedly describes its diseased anatomy and how it has affected the black community as the 'syphilis that has eaten to the core' of Zimbabwe.[14]

Marechera and Shelley are not easy writers by any stretch of the imagination. Their writings are dialogues within dialogues and dialogues with other writings and philosophies and thinking. This is an important anarchic strategy, a critical model in which no set hierarchy exists. Their writings become amalgams of different genres, in which linear links are broken. The narratives cascade in no apparent or necessary order: there is dialogue by the characters; allusions to philosophy and myths; dialogue between characters within the narrative and larger contemporary issues persisting at the time of composition. Just as in everyday experience, the implication here is that everyone must confront a variety of ways of learning and living. There is, indeed, a kind of exuberant anarchy in this process. No firm authority exists in the text. There seems to be no overarching authorial demand. The open ending invites the reader to pursue further conversations as well as to go beyond the text into conversations that Shelley and Marechera do not chart. So, the reader can and must piece together an interpretation of the amalgamated elements and discover what other questions could be asked.

Therefore the major anarchic concern of their literature is to challenge the tyranny of reason and all that such tyranny implies. What is required is a demanding moral and intellectual rigor to keep alert the evidence of a need for reconsideration and alteration of our point of view in the light of new experiences. Hence, both writers desired freedom from conventions, and from the monotonous, rigid lifestyle of an emerging bourgeois capitalism and a rising political class. It is a freedom from the established order of things, against precise laws and dogma and formulas. This philosophy of defiance

---

[14] Dambudzo Marechera, *The House of Hunger* (1978; London: Heinemann, 2009), 78.

of the conventional and the desire for change, sometimes achieved in a shockingly scandalous fashion, is a prominent characteristic between Marechera and Shelley not only in their works but also in their lives. While they believed that their writings were capable of perpetuating change, what was most remarkable was their ability to induce change within society and individual mentalities, a kind of re-awakening from the slumber of the tediousness and monotony of daily life often regulated by others for profit and/or for power.

Shelley's motivation was invariably the impulse of a desire to define and enhance our humanity. While freedom is individual in its source, it immediately becomes social in its application. Shelley's catalogue of poems is a series of renewed self-criticisms and analyses, a continuously dramatized process of self understanding. And Marechera was convinced that individuals within society were prevented from conceiving things in new ways because of their reverence and unsuspecting respect for the established order. He eloquently records this disappointment in the 'journal' section of *Mindblast* where he writes:

> I felt no group sense and no group context with all those around me, London or Harare. There was just this terrifying sense of having missed the bus of human motion, having missed out on whatever all these and others had which made them look 'at home' in the world.[15]

History has shown that holding onto tradition does not allow society to move forward. It is always the case that dominant social powers with their hegemonic influences prevent individuals from living as they are meant to, in a spontaneous fashion. What is apparently clear is that traditional thoughts are artificial ideas established by those holding the most influence.

While the largely European scholarship that has grown around Marechera in recent years insistently characterizes him

---

[15] Dambudzo Marechera, *Mindblast, or, The Definitive Buddy* (Harare: College Press, 1984), 120.

as a 'madman,' a writer with 'no message,' the evidence of his literary works shows that he had similar desires as Shelley to reform his society's attitude. In order to communicate their ambitious literary visions, both writers saw the need for aesthetic reform. The level of experimentation and the dexterity of their writings suggest that Marechera and Shelley felt that the aesthetic ideals in place were far too rigid and lacked emotional intensity, thus their aesthetic standards were defiant and valued spontaneity and unconventional manipulation of genres, subjectivity, and emotional representation. Reality, from an anarchist perspective, is neither rigidly determined nor a shapeless void; it is a vast sum of transformations which can neither be predetermined nor preconceived, a field which is open before human spontaneity.

Reading Shelley alongside Dambudzo Marechera with a comparative objective seems, at face value, presumptuous and contrived. But I would like to conclude that this pairing provides an opportunity to re-read Shelley and Marechera in a larger, global context and challenges the celebrated perceptions of both writers. It is a fact that the two write from out of different historical and social contexts and elaborate different textual strategies in response to their experiences and therefore I posit that their various works can be regarded as variations on a theme. I think they present varieties of the 'Romantic experience' – an intense concern in matters political that arise from the dilemma between the intellectual principles that underlie their political assent and their romantic intuition.

So, a comparison of the two writers is an extension and elaboration of Edward Said's notion of 'discrepant experiences.'[16] For Said, a contrapuntal reading of such 'overlapping and interconnected experiences' enables us

> to think through and interpret together experiences that are discrepant, each with its particular agenda and pace of development,

[16] Edward Said, *Culture and Imperialism* (London: Chatto & Windus, 1992), 35-49.

its own internal formations, its internal coherence and system of external relationships, all of them co-existing and interacting with others.[17]

In bringing together Shelley and Marechera, it is my interpretive aim to make concurrent those views and experiences that have been ideologically and culturally closed to each other, and also rather attempt to highlight other suppressed views and experiences. In this instance, I want to reflect on Shelley's conception of philosophical anarchism and his broader creative goal of revolutionary praxis. With Shelley, there appears two tendencies of anarchist theory. The doctrine shifts from abstract speculation on the use and abuse of political power to a theory of political action enacted in the drama of his poetry. At the same time anarchism ceases to be a political philosophy of the radical petty bourgeoisie and becomes a political doctrine, which looked for the mass of its adherents among workers and ordinary citizens. There is also a sense in which Shelley internationalized his thoughts and ideas to encompass all humanity making himself a citizen of the world. Marechera embraces that concept when he lashes out that he 'would question anyone calling me an African writer. Either you are a writer or you are not. If you are a writer for a specific nation then fuck you.'[18] As Shelley writes of a utopian world, a world yet-to-come, his interpretation of history is doubly prophetic; it offers the possibility of a 'brighter Hellas,' while acknowledging that the menacing presence of tyranny will continue. Marechera in his fiction seeks to unmask the masquerade of post-colonial independence. The questions that Marechera asks with brutal honesty are — how shall we use the immense opening we have gained, which enables us to liberate our minds, our souls, our bodies, and our instincts, from the historical memory embedded in our sub-conscious

[17] Ibid., 36.
[18] Veit-Wild, *Dambudzo Marechera*, 121.

understanding, which instructs us to fear and respect the law and order and social regularities dictated by an unchallengeable Other? What shall we, the emancipated people, define as our own selves? In many instances, the answer to these questions produces the ghastly masquerade of which Shelley writes. In this way, the two were certainly kindred spirits, literary 'buddies.' Their journeys never crossed, but the paths they walked were certainly shared.

The pairing of Marechera and Shelley is therefore not as odd as it might at first seem. There are still issues and creative principles that, despite contexts, are still worthy of debate and discussion. The reason for the persistence and power of anarchism is fundamentally moral. The outrage of individual radicals like Marechera and Shelley, their profound sense of social injustice, comes not from finely honed political or economic theory. It surfaces from a ferment of anger and resentment conjured up by poverty and corruption. This is the realm of the literary anarchist; this is the realm of Dambudzo Marechera and Percy Bysshe Shelley.

2 Blowing People's Minds
Anarchist Thought in Dambudzo Marechera's *Mindblast*

ANIAS MUTEKWA

Reading Marechera's work encourages one to look again at the political philosophy of anarchism. Like Marxism, against which it was conceived, anarchism represents one of those liberatory discourses that were in one way or another linked with the Enlightenment. Its leading proponents were Kropotkin and Bakunin in Russia, Proudhon in France, and Godwin in England. As Pierre-Joseph Proudhon makes clear in his writings, anarchists are opposed to all forms of power, authority and hierarchy.[1] Indeed, one of the defining features of nineteenth-century European anarchism was the way in which the State was regarded as the major source of repression. Unsurprisingly, then, Proudhon and others sought its abolition. Privileging the freedom of the individual, whose instincts and intuitions need to be given free expression rather than limited by the demands and exigencies of the State, anarchism proposes:

> Liberty that consists in the full development of all the material, intellectual and moral powers that are latent in each person; liberty that recognizes no restrictions other than those determined by the laws of our own individual nature, which cannot properly be regarded as restrictions since these laws are not imposed by any outside legislator beside or above us, but are immanent and inherent, forming the very basis of our material, intellectual and moral being ... they do not limit us but are the real and immediate conditions of our freedom.[2]

[1] See, for example, Pierre-Joseph Proudhon, *What is Property?* (1840), ed. Donald Kelley and Bonnie Smith (Cambridge: Cambridge UP, 1994); and Pierre-Joseph Proudhon, *The General Idea of the Revolution in the Nineteenth Century* (1851; New York: Cosimo, 2007).

[2] Mikhail Bakunin, 'The Paris Commune and the Idea of the State' (1871), in *Writings*

For Mikhail Bakunin, such an account of liberty amounts to a political philosophy. But, as French anarchist historian Jean Grave makes clear, there is a distinction to be made between political anarchists and intellectual anarchists – a term that has been used to describe Marechera.[3] While political anarchists follow the political ideal of anarchism, intellectual anarchists are considered 'monsters of the intellectual order' who 'clamor against the philistine, the bourgeois, [and] the reign of money.'[4] More than suggestive of deviancy, such 'monsters' seem to position themselves in opposition to everything in order to try and undermine dominant ways of thinking. Indeed, Christopher Forth explains that in French intellectual discourse at the end of the nineteenth century, 'the charge of intellectual anarchy was leveled against any individual or group threatening to subvert dominant conceptions of intellectual or cultural hierarchy.'[5] As such, the avant-garde artist is always-already an 'intellectual anarchist,' which is to say, a marginalized type of intellectual. Nothing describes Marechera better than this – an intellectual who stood on the margins of both African and European literary and philosophical traditions.

Unsurprisingly, then, anarchist ideas permeate the works of Marechera, none more so than *Mindblast*.[6] Even though it never really gained any significant popularity in African political thought, anarchism sits at the very core of Marechera's splintered political philosophy. While Marxism found expression and sympathy in the works of some leading African writers, most notably Ngugi wa Thiong'o and Sembène Ousmane,

on the Paris Commune: Marx, Engels, Bakunin, Kropotkin, and Lenin (St Petersburg, FL: Red and Black Publishers, 2008), 76.

[3] Flora Veit-Wild, 'Words as Bullets: The Writings of Dambudzo Marechera,' *Zambezia* 14, no. 2 (1987), 113.

[4] Christopher Forth, 'Intellectual Anarchy and Imaginary Otherness: Gender, Class, and Pathology in French Intellectual Discourse, 1890-1900,' *The Sociological Quarterly* 37, no. 4 (Autumn, 2006), 656.

[5] Ibid., 646.

[6] Dambudzo Marechera, *Mindblast, or, The Definitive Buddy* (Harare: College Press, 1984). Unless otherwise indicated, further page references are in the main text.

anarchism rarely did the same. Since it arrived in Africa at a time when the continent was widely engaged in nationalist struggles for liberation, the demand for cultural revitalization, and the process of nation-building, anarchism has rarely been regarded as a viable political philosophy. Indeed, it is wholly antithetical to these collective, nationalist pursuits. As such, it is interesting to note the tension that exists between Marechera's individual anarchist vision and the dominant political ideas sweeping the continent – a politics of national liberation and the recovery of a battered racial pride, which found expression in artistic and political movements such as Négritude. For Marechera, such political movements were deeply flawed. Only anarchist thought could provide the territory for the 'literary shock treatment' necessary to jolt people from the slumber produced by what he saw as the soporific ideologies and Enlightenment-originated modernist meta-narratives that diluted the political consciousness of the Zimbabwean people.[7]

So it is that elements of the political philosophy of anarchism are to be found in *Mindblast*. In *Mindblast*, Marechera exposes the murky relationship between representative government and authoritarianism, oppression, and corruption by centering on a critique of power. In the drama sketches under the title, 'The Skin of Time: plays by Buddy,' the post-independence rulers are portrayed as fast-becoming the colonialists they have replaced. Similarly, the authoritarian and oppressive tendencies of those in power are hinted at in the drama sketch, 'The Coup.' One character, Spotty, pointedly remarks, 'I forgot that those above us seldom look down to see where they put their feet' (12). This aside from a seemingly defeated person resonates well with the anarchist critique of all forms of representative authority – that representation is simply another mask for the oppression of the governed. Spotty goes further, highlighting the complicity of the people in their own oppression. Explaining how a

---

[7] Flora Veit-Wild, *Writing Madness: Borderlines of the Body in African Literature* (Harare: Weaver Press; Oxford: James Currey, 2006), 62.

sense of awe, hero-worship, and a deeply worrying uncritical subservience to authority characterizes 'the masses,' Spotty announces, 'That is how the lean spotty silent majority becomes the composite heap upon which criminal tyranny flourishes' (12). It is an apposite remark about the condition of the newly emerged independent nation of Zimbabwe.

Much of the literature of the period is celebratory, rejoicing in the act of winning independence. However, Marechera's writing exposes the empty rhetoric of what the majority of Zimbabweans thought of as 'The People's Government.' If anything, as Drake exemplifies with his heroic exploits that although seemingly noble are in fact merely a means to win the heart of his girlfriend (14), selfishness more than the sacrosanct ideals of freedom and national liberation often mediates the consciousness of the people and informs the actions of those in authority. The pessimism expressed here links *Mindblast* with other texts from around Africa, such as Ngugi's *A Grain of Wheat* (1967) and Ayi Kwei Armah's *The Beautyful Ones are Not Yet Born* (1968), and so hints that such selfishness is common among the continent's new leaders. This hint is written large in Marechera's surrealist sketch, 'Grimknife Junior and Rix the Giant Cat.' Selfishness becomes self-serving aggression as the post-independent State is seen as not only totalitarian but also predatory – preying on the very people that it has liberated. In this way, the State is responsible for continuing the victim/victimizer paradigm between governors and the governed. The trinity that summarizes the ruling class's ideology 'patriotism, loyalty and responsibility' (52), sacrosanct though it might appear, is revealed as merely masking the ruling class's intention of blinding and exploiting the people.

Marechera also identifies the operation of culture as another site of control. Understanding that the particular version of culture called 'national culture,' so readily employed in the discourse of nation-building, is used to privilege a non-oppositional collective mythology and thereby suppress other ways of thinking, Marechera writes of the artist Buddy. Buddy quickly realizes that his voice, which is discordant to that of the cultural nationalists, is silenced. It is the product of a State that makes the connection between 'disruptions in the realm of the intellection' and 'all other forms of social disorder.'[8] As the nineteenth-century French philosopher Auguste Comte notes,

> So long as individual minds do not assent to a certain number of general ideas forming a common social doctrine, there is no hiding the fact that the state of nations will remain revolutionary, in spite of all political palliatives, and that institutions will remain only provisional.[9]

It is in the interest of the State, then, to ensure that its citizens think in the same way about the same things. Marechera makes the point explicit through Grimknife Junior, who is arrested because 'he thinks and acts as he wishes rather than in terms of what society has validated.'[10] During Grimknife's interrogation at the hands of Rix, the Re-orientation Officer makes clear that he is determined to turn Grimknife into what the State considers to be a 'useful citizen.' That is, 'someone who does what he is told. Someone who says exactly what others say' (45). In this way, Marechera paints the post-independence government as repressive and oppressive, the only escape from which is the liberation of the individual from all kinds of limitation. To this end, Marechera promotes the Bohemian lifestyle that he lives on the streets of Harare.

The Marechera-type narrator who leads a bohemian life in Harare attracts the label 'anarchist.' Since his life-style is at odds with the needs of society – social commitment, conformity, economic productivity, and so on – the State seeks to limit the

[8] Forth, 'Intellectual Anarchy,' 648.
[9] Auguste Comte, *The Essential Comte*, ed. Stanislav Andreski (New York: Harper and Row, 1974), 37.
[10] Patrizia Perocchio, 'A Black Insider: The Man Walking Away From His Shadow,' in *Emerging Perspectives on Dambudzo Marechera*, eds. Flora Veit-Wild and Anthony Chennells (Trenton, NJ: Africa World Press, 1999), 212.

freedom of the individual to live his life as he sees fit. Clearly, Marechera writes against this process of limitation; and it is his anarchist vision that provides the provocative dimension to his writing that encourages his readers to engage in a critical re-examination of society in order to stall its seemingly inevitable fall into the void of totalization and essentialism. Like Buddy, the narrator is revolted by the materialist culture that marks life in the postcolony. For Buddy, his refusal to conform is evident of his self-liberation from all that is organized against the true freedom of the individual, a condition which resonates with the anarchist belief that only the individual can liberate him or herself. Leadership, if any, should be by example and this example is what Buddy tries to show to those around him. Buddy rejects the label 'anarchist' in the text because it is used to position him as the Other, and consequently to marginalize him. 'There was so much more to man than the petty regulations of nation and society provided for,' he states, 'but if you expressed that, they called you an anarchist' (63). A little later it becomes clear that while society's petty regulations might be unavoidable, they cannot be considered an end in themselves. It is continuous metamorphosis, Marechera seems to say, that is the key to real progress, real freedom.

There is a problem with this understanding of the anarchist agenda, though. Such anarchist thought is part of the modernist meta-narratives of the Enlightenment. In place of the rational, logical, and scientific subject it composes 'the natural man,' a rather appealing but nonetheless fictitious writing of man. It is this that limits the liberatory potential of this kind of anarchism since, like other grand narratives, it is ultimately reductionist, glossing over the pluralities of a life. This, though, is not all that Marechera has to offer on anarchist thought.

In the context of a post-independent Zimbabwe where realism and socialist realism were the privileged aesthetic ideologies of the State,[11] Marechera produced *Mindblast*. It was

---

[11] See Emmanuel Ngara, *Art and Ideology in the African Novel: A Study of the Influence of*

the work of an individual thinker who espoused individual thoughts. In this, Marechera consciously aligned himself with writers such as Soyinka and Armah rather than those who he thought of as simply producing social realist novels. Talking of his association to Soyinka and Armah, Marechera explains:

> The three of us are always seen as individualists, and this word is used in an insulting way. If people accuse you of individualism, then they are actually saying you are reactionary, you are capitalist in your approach to art, you are not a writer of the people.[12]

It is this kind of pronouncement of individualism that leads critics such as Flora Veit-Wild and Rino Zhuwarara to think of Marechera as an 'intellectual anarchist,' as a writer that is suspicious of any movement towards the collective. Through his writing he intended to jolt his readers from the complacency that had arrived as a consequence of their subjection to the prevailing soporific discourses of the State. Part of his strategy for doing so was to subvert the English language.

To begin with, English, as the language of the colonizer, needed taming in order to carry the weight of his experiences as a colonial and postcolonial subject. By reducing the language and everything 'to its ultimate last components,' Marechera believed it would 'blow people's minds.'[13] The image that Marechera encourages here is that of the bomb, of the explosion, and with it the modality by which he intended to liberate people from their slumber. What he calls for is the forceful detonation of the limp ideas and concepts that circulate in the minds of people. But after this moment of destruction, the result will be that rare thing – something entirely 'new.' This is what the title of *Mindblast* attempts to portray. This is

---

Marxism on the African Novel (Oxford: Heinemann, 1985).

[12] Alle Lansu, 'Escape from the "House of Hunger:" Marechera Talks about His Life,' in *Dambudzo Marechera: A Source Book on his Life and Work*, by Flora Veit-Wild (London: Hans Zell, 1992), 44.

[13] Flora Veit-Wild, *Dambudzo Marechera: A Source Book on his Life and Work*, 220.

Marechera's cure for the 'brain death' that he saw as the major problem in the Zimbabwean postcolony. The prescription is conceived in the anarchist tradition in the sense that the destruction is set in place without a clear blueprint for how to proceed afterwards.

In any case, *Mindblast* certainly inherits the aura of intellectual revolt in Europe, which Marechera witnessed first-hand. Lauding the rejection of materialism and conventional intellectualism sweeping across Europe in the 1970s, Marechera sees himself as part of

> that generation which had tasted the excitement of individual freedom and collective health in body and mind and environment … a generation that had been caught up in the search for spiritual and inner development and rejected intellectualism and the middle-class ambitions of its parents. (60)

Some of that 'excitement' arrived through the aggressive new approaches to literature becoming popular in the 1970s. Clearly, poststructuralism and the emergent ideas of postmodernism struck a profound chord with Marechera; and all his work seems to bear the traces of this kind of thinking. In addition, though, it also seems that the way in which these new kinds of thinking forced a revision of nineteenth-century anarchist philosophy interested Marechera. At the very least, the intersection encouraged people to revisit the work of Friedrich Nietzsche as they sought to understand the dynamics, affects, and effects of thinking through 'the death of God.' Indeed, Nietzsche was important to Marechera because, as Lewis Call suggests,

> Nietzsche's thinking lays waste to every received truth of the modern world, including those of science, politics and religion. His philosophy is thus anarchist in the strong sense of the term: it includes important elements of an anarchist politics.[14]

---

[14] Lewis Call, *Postmodern Anarchism* (Boston: Lexington Books, 2002), 2.

Indeed, it is the way in which Nietzsche attacks Enlightenment ideas of subjectivity that gives rise to what postmodern
anarchists refer to as the 'anarchy of the subject.' It is an
observation that 'the postmodern subject is and must remain
multiple, dispersed, and (as Gilles Deleuze would have it)
schizophrenic.'[15] This anarchy of the subject is evident in
Marechera's writing, which is largely autobiographical but
nevertheless contains frequent reinventions that fictionalize
his life beyond the autobiographical. This gives rise to what
Melissa Levin and Laurice Taitz call 'fictional autobiographies
and autobiographical fictions.'[16] In *Mindblast*, these multiple
selves are evident in Marechera's fictional selves – Grimknife
Junior and Buddy. Yet, another 'fictional autobiography' and
'autobiographical fiction' is contained in 'From the Journal'
in the 'Appendix' of *Mindblast*. Here, Marechera casts his life
as one underwritten by multiple and shifting identities and
subjectivities. In so doing he also undermines the notion
of truth as an essential quality, and positions it as a mere
construction of various transient subjectivities. All identities,
as Marechera shows, are always in a state of flux. It is something
that resonates deeply with the Nietzschean concept of the
'anarchy of becoming,' whereby the postmodern anarchist

> must engage in a project of self-overcoming. By constantly re-
> radicalizing the subject, by constantly immersing the 'self' in the
> river of becoming, the Nietzschean anarchist evades the possibility
> that her subjectivity will re-crystallize in a totalizing fashion.[17]

This is what Marechera shows through his shifting subjectivities
and identities. The narrator Buddy is thus invariably revolted
by the materialist culture that pervades life in Harare as it
consigns a single subjectivity that is the very opposite of life

---

[15] Ibid., 22.
[16] Melissa Levin and Laurice Taitz, 'Fictional Autobiographies or Autobiographical
Fictions?' in *Emerging Perspectives on Dambudzo Marechera*, 163.
[17] Call, *Postmodern Anarchism*, 22.

and freedom as viewed from the contemporary anarchist perspective. Here, difference becomes constructed as insanity and Buddy is thus regarded as 'insane to pursue something that did not generate money' (60). The identities and subjectivities that the fictional selves see in Harare are, therefore, the very same 'crystallizations' and 'totalizations' that Call mentions. However, Marechera's protest writing, even his private life, negates the totalization and essentialism of identities and subjectivities that he sees as the very bane of the postcolony.

In *Mindblast* the single subjectivity that the African cultural nationalists are trying to construct is exposed through the surrealist sketch of 'Grimknife Junior and Rix the Giant Cat.' That is to say, Grimknife and Buddy expose the attempt of the State to suppress the proliferation of 'non-productive' subjectivities. But, Grimknife's and Buddy's 'anarchy of becoming' refuses to crystallize into a coherent form. Such an 'anarchy of becoming' allows everything to be understood as a process rather than a product, and so the State's claim that the revolution has been successful, that the process of liberation is completed, is greeted with a fundamental skepticism. Such pronouncements are regarded as an attempt to silence other competing discourses. They also give rise to a sense of creeping totalitarianism, which is alluded to in *Mindblast* through the experiences of Buddy and Grimknife Junior. Rather prophetically, then, *Mindblast* anticipates Robert Mugabe's attempt to introduce a one-party State in Zimbabwe in the 1980s, and the polarization of the nation's body-politic into 'patriots' and 'sell-outs' at the turn of the millennium. Both actions can only be seen as the attempt to craft a singular, privileged subjectivity of the Zimbabwean people through the marginalization and ultimate silencing of dissenting voices.

At every level, Marechera's *Mindblast* resists this unifying project. Structurally, *Mindblast* is a menippean novel. That is to say, it defies the edicts of conventional literary genres. By collapsing the boundaries between drama, prose, and poetry, it refuses the reader's initial instinct to categorize it. In the words of Drew Shaw, 'Since the menippean novel can take on any number of forms, it possesses a metamorphic quality which enables it to transgress a host of barriers and boundaries, including that of nationality.'[18] It is this metamorphic quality, then, that lends itself well to Marechera's aim of resisting the State's unifying project.

The morphology of the book's structure finds itself repeated in the text. *Mindblast* moves away from a conception of a mono-lithic subjectivity by privileging metamorphosis as the only quality that ensures progress and the liberation of the individual. So it is that the content of the text signifies open-endedness and flux, rather than closure and, ultimately, fossilization. An acceptance of plurality and difference is thus brought to the fore in the text through the satirical depiction of life in Harare.

The common charge that *Mindblast* works against 'the real' in order to problematize the almost naturalized discourses of nationalism and imperialism links Marechera's political thought with postmodern anarchism. Indeed, it seems he shares a particular affinity with French philosopher Jean Baudrillard, whose 'antirealist theory of simulation undermines the "real" subject of modern political discourse, the "real" rationality of that subject, and all "real" political or economic systems founded upon such rational subjectivity.'[19] While Baudrillard undermines the 'real' via simulation, Marechera does so through the operation of surrealism. As Stephen Slemon notes, the aesthetic ideology of surrealism is one in which a sustained opposition between realism and its opposite 'forestalls the possibility of interpretive closure through any act of naturalizing the text to an established system of representation.'[20] In this way, *Mindblast* is a profoundly open text. It envisages a mental

---

[18] Drew Shaw, 'Transgressing Traditional Narrative Form,' in *Emerging Perspectives on Dambudzo Marechera*, 14.

[19] Call, *Postmodern Anarchism*, 94.

[20] Stephen Slemon, 'Magic Realism as Postcolonial Discourse,' in *Magic Realism: Theory, History, Community*, Lois Parkinson Zamora and Wendy B. Faris (eds) (Durham: Duke UP, 1995), 410.

revolution as the only way to recreate and revitalize the world. Marechera's 'mindblast' is conceived of in the same terms that Call talks of Baudrillard's revolutionary agenda. He writes,

> What Baudrillard is talking about is a theoretical, analytic, interpretive violence of thought rather than deed, a violence which cheerfully murders concepts, ideas and semiotic structures.[21]

There can be no better way of describing Marechera's attempt to hasten our desire to 'reprogram or redesign ourselves'[22] in defiance of the parameters set by the State. *Mindblast* encourages us to begin this reprogramming, to begin the process of distancing ourselves from the thought-forms of the State.

In addition to his anarchist perspective, Dambudzo Marechera, because of his experiences in Zimbabwe and England, is the archetypal postcolonial exile – a hybrid figure gifted with the incisive second sight of one who is looking back at his nation from a distance. Indeed, Marechera's exilic status positions him as both 'insider' and 'outsider' to the various discourses – colonial, metropolitan, nationalist – that he critiques in *Mindblast*. Marechera's rejection of cultural nationalism and his privileging of pluralities and multiple subjectivities are undoubtedly the fruit of such hybridity – the product of multiple influences that have shaped him. His second sight enables him to see beyond the homogenizing drives of such discourses, and therefore allows him to concentrate on the significant emergent condition of class division in the early post-independence period. So, for example, in 'Blitzkrieg,' the character Alfie, as the author's mouthpiece, laments the fact that 'there are many shades of black but the only true one is that of the have-nots' (37). In the same vein, the narrator of 'The Prologue' is able to lament the fact that there is no discernible difference between the old order and the new order in the postcolony. Talking about the history

---

[21] Call, *Postmodern Anarchism*, 108.
[22] Ibid., 52.

of Harare, the narrator says, 'the white settlers had created it as a frontier town for gold and lust, lurid adventures and ruthless rule. The black inheritors had not changed that – just the name' (51). It is a biting critique of post-independence Zimbabwe that evidences Marechera's continuing concern for the people of his nation. Moreover, it is evidence that Marechera put much stall in the idea that profound revolution finds its quarry in the everyday. In this way, his 'one man revolution,' his 'one man liberation,' echoes the sentiment that sits at the core of Murray Bookchin's political philosophy:

> It is plain that the goal of revolution today is the liberation of daily life ... Any revolution that fails to achieve that goal is counterrevolution. Above all, it is *we* who have to be liberated, *our* daily lives, with all their moments, hours and days, and not universals like 'History' and 'Society.'[23]

In this way, Marechera and many of the narrators in his texts take charge of their lives and free themselves to live as they wish, not as society dictated. So from the general anti-hegemonic position of the postcolonial, Marechera moves down to the level of the (splintered) individual that postmodern anarchism privileges.

So, Marechera, the typical postcolonial exilic writer, was neither a 'heretic,' 'the man who betrayed Africa,' nor even a simple 'dissident.' As an individual he accepted the multiple influences that had impacted on his upbringing, and used them in order to critique what he saw as a failing State. In this way, *Mindblast* shows that Marechera was not simply an 'intellectual anarchist.' Rather, he was a socially committed writer who recognized the inability to find true liberation in all the universal narratives that claimed to emancipate the enslaved. What *Mindblast* shows us, then, is that true liberation, 'freedom,' can only arrive at a cost – the cost of a comfortable, familiar, mild life.

[23] Murray Bookchin, *Post-Scarcity Anarchism* (Berkeley: Ramparts Press, 1971), 44.

3 Grotesque Intimacies
Embodiment & the Spirit of Violence in 'House of Hunger'

ANNA-LEENA TOIVANEN

In her widely-cited review of *The House of Hunger*,[1] Juliet Okonkwo criticizes the debut writer Dambudzo Marechera for self-purposefully subjecting his readers to a grotesque imagery:

> Marechera deliberately presents actions that are sordid and shocking. The vulgarity and histrionic nature of many of them, the excessive interest in sex activity, his tireless attempt to rake up filth, his insistent expression of debased philosophy built around 'stains on a sheet' and which is given expression in the words 'What [else] is there?', put this volume among avant-garde art that is characteristic of modern European culture. All this is alien to Africa – a continent of hope and realizable dreams.[2]

Okonkwo goes on to object to Marechera's abundant and apparently haphazard use of 'obscene and four-letter words,' which, as she maintains, 'are used purely for their own sake.'[3] Okonkwo's critique is emblematic in the sense that it articulates the discrepancy between the African nation-building ethos and Marechera's disillusioned postcolonial poetics. While several critics maintained that *The House of Hunger* witnessed Marechera's writerly talent, if not ingenuity[4] – this is something that even Okonkwo suggests in her review – the novella obviously did not meet the demands of contemporary political

---

[1] Dambudzo Marechera, *The House of Hunger* (1978; Oxford: Heinemann, 1993). Unless otherwise indicated, further page references are in the main text.

[2] Juliet Okonkwo, 'A Review of *The House of Hunger*,' *Okike: An African Journal of New Writing* (June 1981), 91.

[3] Ibid., 91.

[4] For an account of the critical acclaim of the novella, see Flora Veit-Wild, *Dambudzo Marechera: A Source Book on his Life and Work* (London: Hans Zell, 1992), 186-91.

agendas that had their bearing on the conception of literature. Okonkwo's words convey the great expectations and hopes set in independence, suggesting simultaneously that, in the face of such a great collective liberatory effort, there is something truly inappropriate in Marechera's violently grotesque approach. Indeed, Okonkwo's words capture the spirit of African post-independence dogmas with their requirements of a clearly articulated political writerly commitment in line with the aesthetic standards of social realism.[5] Marechera himself, in contrast, believed in the power of 'scandalous and eccentric' imagery in destabilizing the current order of things and in envisioning newness,[6] and developed his grotesque, embodied aesthetics according to this insight. On the African literary scene, Marechera is certainly not alone in relying on grotesque imagery; several writers before and after him have used it as a vehicle of critical consciousness directed against the injustices and imbalances of power and wealth on the continent especially in the post-independence context. For instance, Wole Soyinka's *The Interpreters* (1965), Ngugi wa Thiong'o's *Devil on the Cross* (1982), Ayi Kwei Armah's *The Beautyful Ones Are Not Yet Born* (1968), and Zakes Mda's *Ways of Dying* (1995) can be seen to represent the postcolonial African literary grotesque, which has been particularly fascinated with the consuming body in terms of eating and digestion. As the following analysis suggests, Marechera's work evokes the notion of grotesque primarily through physical violence and sex.

In this chapter, I address the condition of banalized violence that is omnipresent in 'House of Hunger,' with specific focus on the ways in which it manifests itself in the intimacy of embodied encounters. My analysis is informed by Mikhail Bakhtin's notion of grotesque as well as Achille Mbembe's

[5] See Gerald Gaylard, *After Colonialism: African Postmodernism and Magical Realism* (Johannesburg: Witwatersrand UP, 2006), 30-31.
[6] Dambudzo Marechera, 'The African Writer's Experience of European Literature,' *Zambezia* 14, no. 2 (1987), 101.

theorization on the postcolonial aesthetics of vulgarity. Further, I argue that the persistent question posed by the novella's characters, 'What else is there?', interpreted by Okonkwo as a mere manifestation of Marechera's 'stains on a sheet' poetics, articulates an elusive, almost disbelieving hope for something else or something new that is incongruent with the masculinist anti-colonial independence ambitions. Analyzing Marechera's characters, confined to the all-encompassing vortex of violence and in the abject materiality of their violated and violating bodies, I will also contemplate the possibility of reading the Marecheran grotesque as a resistance strategy that challenges both the colonial order and its anti-colonial, nationalist sequel.

The body, and particularly its 'dirty' and bruise-prone qualities, manifests strongly its presence throughout 'House of Hunger.' Already the word 'hunger' in the title, with its connotations to eating as a material bodily function and not solely as a spiritual striving for something out of reach, is illustrative of the emphasis on grotesque embodiment. On the whole, Marechera's interest in the purely material side of corporeality represents an ironic reappropriation of the colonial attitude of reducing the colonized to a mere body-thing without subjectivity.[7] However, it might be more fruitful to discuss Marechera's notion of embodiment in the light of Mikhail Bakhtin's writings on the grotesque.

According to Bakhtin, the grotesque body is characterized by the way in which it transgresses its own limits and opens up to the world.[8] In this respect, the grotesque puts specific emphasis on those parts of the body that either enable it to be entered, or that stick out from it – the mouth, nose, belly, genitalia, and anus. Consequently, the grotesque is fascinated with different bodily functions such as eating, sexual intercourse, giving

---

[7] Achille Mbembe, *On the Postcolony*, trans. A. M. Berrett, et al. (Berkeley: University of California Press, 2001), 27; 187.

[8] Mikhail Bakhtin, *Rabelais and His World*, trans. Hélène Iswolsky (Bloomington: Indiana UP, 1984), 281.

birth, vomiting, urinating, defecating, or mauling and tearing the body, as well as in the excretion related to the mentioned functions.[9] Another central feature in the grotesque body is that it is marked by ambivalence; it is in an endless state of transformation, denoting the co-existence of the old and the new.[10] The ambivalent dimension of the grotesque entails transgression of fixed categories and fluctuation between entities that may conventionally be seen as mutually exclusive; ambivalence marks the uneasy and disturbing quality of the grotesque as it violates conventional boundaries. Finally, the power of the grotesque lies in its ability to challenge the present state of affairs and to engender a new vision of the world.

While Bakhtin's notion of the grotesque builds on the idea of resisting the dominant culture through the low and ridicule, Achille Mbembe, in his re-appropriation of the concept to the African post-independence context, suggests that the grotesque is more likely based on the logic of 'conviviality' that 'inscribe[s] the dominant and the dominated within the same *episteme*.'[11] Mbembe's reformulation shifts the focus from the Bakhtinian dynamism of high/low and domination/resistance to a more subtle, less binaristic understanding of postcolonial complicity. For Mbembe, the aesthetics of vulgarity is an inherent element of authoritarian postcolonial *commandement* regimes. From this it follows that by engaging with grotesque imagery, the embodied postcolonial subjects do not simply resist but also *represent* the operation of power.[12] In a similar vein, my reading of the Marecheran grotesque entails less an emphasis on straightforward counter-discursivity than on the idea that the embodied grotesque in the novella is an articulation of the (post-)colonial condition that writes itself on the intimacy of the bodies, engaging them, hence, in bearing

---

[9] Ibid., 26.
[10] Ibid., 206.
[11] Mbembe, *On the Postcolony*, 110.
[12] Ibid., 128-9.

witness to the operations of power. This witnessing occurs in spite of the subjects, although the level of intention is not of course the issue here.

The narrative present of 'House of Hunger' is set in the years of the anti-colonial freedom struggle at the end of the 1970s. The novella articulates the spirit of violence that marks Zimbabwe's transition from a minority ruled settler colony into an independent postcolony. This particular spirit of violence, in Mbembe's definition, 'makes the violence omnipresent; it is presence – presence not deferred ... but spatialized, visible, immediate, sometimes ritualized, sometimes dramatic, very often caricatural.'[13] Indeed, in Zimbabwe, the last years of the freedom struggle were marked by the omnipresence of violence, up to the extent that it became 'a daily occurrence, always possible, always unpredictable, always at close quarters.'[14] It turned out to be extremely difficult to break this vicious circle at the arrival of independence – and even far beyond independence, as a glimpse of the country's twenty-first century political violence suggests.[15] This overwhelming and diversiform presence of violence is exemplified throughout 'House of Hunger.' While the novella's contextual setting is in the most intense years of the long freedom war period, the actual struggle remains on the fringes of the narrative. The violent reality of the war surfaces most explicitly in paragraphs that depict the display of the dead guerillas' bodies (3, 60). The decaying corpses are stripped of heroic connotations and invested with plainly grotesque material meanings: 'The corpses looked as if they had been dead for quite a while. One face seemed to be nothing but a mass of flies' (61). Moreover, no-one seems to be shocked at the face of these grotesque

---

[13] Ibid., 175.

[14] Jane Parpart, 'Masculinities, Race and Violence in the Making of Zimbabwe,' in *Manning the Nation: Father Figures in Zimbabwean Literature and Society*, eds Kizito Z. Muchemwa and Robert Muponde (Harare: Weaver, 2007), 112.

[15] David Kaulemu, 'The Culture of Party Politics and the Concept of the State,' in *Zimbabwe: The Past is the Future*, ed. David Harold-Barry (Harare: Weaver, 2004), 81.

displays; rather, the macabre details seem to fascinate the spectators. Instead of being represented as a controllable, heroic-prone means serving a liberating communal end, 'House of Hunger' portrays violence as a cumulative and self-nourishing, somewhat banalized force whose potential threat realizes itself almost at any occasion. The atmosphere is heavy with the spirit of violence, the colonized condition being primarily defined by hatred for 'the bloody whites,' inciting them to 'spoil … for a fight' (2) like the anonymous narrator's aggressive brother, Peter. On the other hand, some of the characters (including the indigenous king Lobengula), as the narrator maintains, are willingly positioning themselves as victims to be 'eaten' as if bowing to the inevitable (44). This deep-seated dynamism of hatred also motivates the wider social processes of decolonization and nation-building, 'As it [the hatred] swelled and cracked into green life I felt my nation tremble, tremble in the throes of birth – and burst out bloom and branch' (17). The image of a seed of hatred that the narrator buries and waters in his mind is analogous to the processes of decolonization and nation-building. This is a trope that effectively interweaves the private intimacy of the body to the surrounding social developments, transgressing thus the wavering boundary between the private and the public.

Besides the harsh realities of Rhodesian settler rule, a gnawing disbelief in the potentiality of a true liberation nourishes further aggressiveness, 'The freedom we craved for … was so alive in our breath and in our fingers that one became intoxicated by it even before one had actually found it' (3). The deep-rooted disbelief in change finds its articulation in the notion of 'gut-rot' which makes everything turn 'into a stinking horror' (30), that is to say, into 'white shit' (59). At the core of the disillusionment lies the idea of having lost not only the past but also the future: 'There's armies of worms slithering in our history. And there's squadrons of mosquitoes homing

down onto the cradle of our future' (59). The melancholic loss
of a meaningful past and a future worth anticipating results in
a desperate search for 'Black Heroes;' a notion that does not
necessarily refer to freedom fighters or some glorious, already
established figures from Zimbabwe's history. Such Black Heroes
stand for a dream of delivering both the past and the future
from the yoke of colonialism – a dream whose feasibility is
profoundly questioned by the novella. Ultimately, the narrator
loses his patience with finding a proper hero as he grasps that the
time is more favorable for 'the absurd, the grotesque' (29). The
grotesque reduces the temporal axis into a material, embodied
'now-ness;' the past and especially the future are beyond reach
in this configuration of time. Understanding the impossibility
of a future worth anticipating turns the original, yearning
question into a new form, 'Where are the *bloody* heroes?' (29,
43; emphasis added). The answer to this reformulated question
rings with a grotesque, crudely material register. Heroes are
described to have become 'tainted' and 'sullied' (53), or just
mere 'hideous stains,' leaving the disbelieving narrator only
'the genitals of senile gods' to look up to (45–6). Simply
the fact that someone, or, more specifically, Immaculate – a
woman – dares to hope for a change, an elsewhere instead of
the grotesque here-and-nowness, infuriates the disillusioned
narrator, 'And the holy bitch still dreamed, still hoped, still saw
visions – why!' (17).

As Huma Ibrahim has pointed out in her inspiring essay, the
notions of hope and disillusionment in 'House of Hunger' are
profoundly gendered:

> Marechera's invocational cry for the 'black heroes' begins to
> sound … like a hysterical sexo-political evasion. As the men are
> screaming to be redeemed by the non-existent 'black heroes,' the
> women are dreaming of change.[16]

---

[16] Huma Ibrahim, 'The Violated Universe: Neo-Colonial Sexual and Political Consciousness in Dambudzo Marechera,' *Research in African Literatures* 21, no. 2 (1990), 83.

As suggested by Ibrahim, men, while acknowledging the necessity to dream, are 'unable to stand the beauty and idealism of the women's vision.'[17] As the narrator puts it, 'She made me want to dream, made me believe in visions, in hope. But the rock and grit of the earth denied this' (12). When the narrator asks his brother about Immaculate's dreams and hopes, the brother's laconic answer reads simply, 'What she gets' (8). This answer subjects dreams to the crude materiality of the here-and-now which is also the realm of the grotesque. Elsewhere, a white artist with whom the narrator is involved, says, 'Let's both get out of this,' trying to convince the narrator that 'getting out' is 'easy.' The narrator, however, instead of taking this proposal seriously, takes recourse in disillusioned excuses, 'I – the fool! – shook my head sadly and told her parrot-fashion all the good reasons for my not "getting out of this"' (72). This masculinized despondency – imposing its frustrations with the loss of 'authentic black heroes' on women[18] – lays the foundation for the omnipotent, banalized violence that inscribes itself on the bodies of characters in 'House of Hunger.' In this sense, it can be argued that 'House of Hunger' transgresses the boundaries between the private and the public. Embodiment for Marechera represents 'a template for social reality, so that his narrative of post-independence Zimbabwe is in a very real sense "written on the body".'[19] With no way out of the hopelessness and with practically no room for (male) dreams, it seems that 'House of Hunger' becomes captured by the grotesque, crudely material immediacy of the body. Illustrative of this intertwinement between the desperate hope for something else and the grotesque materiality of the violated body is a paragraph where an

[17] Ibid., 84.

[18] For an excellent study on the intersections of gender, embodiment, and nation-building in the postcolonial context see Elleke Boehmer, *Stories of Women: Gender and Narrative in the Postcolonial Nation* (Manchester: Manchester UP, 2005).

[19] Jane Bryce, 'Inside/out: Body and Sexuality in Dambudzo Marechera's Fiction,' in *Emerging Perspectives on Dambudzo Marechera*, ed. Flora Veit-Wild and Anthony Chennells (Trenton, NJ: Africa World Press, 1999), 222.

image of a boy repeating the well-trodden question 'What else is there?' is paralleled with an image of him being beaten up, 'wallowing in his own blood' (65). The question of an elsewhere, a beyond, is also paralleled with an image of the blood-stained shirt of his batterer 'which seemed in outline to be a map of Rhodesia' (65). It seems that in 'House of Hunger,' transgressing the strict boundaries of colonial and post-colonial conditions is only possible within the realm of embodiment, more specifically, in how the boundaries of the body are loosed.

In 'House of Hunger,' grotesque aspects of corporeality find their manifestations on several levels. First of all, there is the thematic of defecating and excrement – which Okonkwo partly refers to in her critique as the author's excessive use of 'four-letter words.' In postcolonial African literatures, excremental language and interest in scatology is a commonly used devise. As Joshua Esty maintains, shit is often their 'governing trope.'[20] While the turn to scatology is closely linked to disillusionment with decolonization and nationalist politics, it also signals a counter-discursive attitude towards the notion of cleanness so fundamental in the development of modernization and colonialism.[21] In this sense, the critical edge of scatology is essentially twofold. For instance, in comparison to Ayi Kwei Armah's novel *The Beautyful Ones Are Not Yet Born*, the shit observed in 'House of Hunger' is not the overriding aspect of the grotesque; Marechera is primarily interested in its sexual/ violent dimensions. Still, the thematic of shit and defecation surfaces frequently throughout the novella. Besides the notion of 'white shit,' also black people and politics in general are considered mere shit (67). Further, there are several more or less metaphorical visits to the toilets (11, 19, 25, 39, 58) and farting connotations (9, 23, 33, 38). At one point, one of the characters even gets 'baptized' in shit during his journalistic

[20] Joshua Esty, 'Excremental Postcolonialism,' *Contemporary Literature* 41, no. 1 (1999), 23.
[21] Ibid., 25.

duties, 'I was writing an article about shantytown and while inspecting the pit-latrines there I fell into the filthy hole' (58). This renders implicit, in a very concrete manner, the intellectual's complicity in (post-)colonial degradation. His good intentions in exposing the decay of his society to the public ends up ridiculed – turned to shit. At one point, the narrator and his friend Harry are in a beer hall, when the latter starts to brag about his white girlfriend, posing the narrator the question that occurs repeatedly throughout the text, 'What else is there, man?' (12). In answering his own rhetorical question, Harry's arm

> swept the panorama of barbed wire, whitewashed houses, drunks, prostitutes, the angelic choirs of god-created flies, and the dust that erupted into little clouds of divine grace wherever the golden sunlight deigned to strike. His god-like gesture stopped abruptly – pointing straight at the stinking public lavatory. (11)

Here, the narrator brings together elements from the conflicting categories of high/low by juxtaposing Western religious imagery with the surrounding Rhodesian reality, eventually ending up at the repulsive smell of the toilets. This captures the critical power of the grotesque outlined in Esty's account, suggesting that everything begins and ends in excrement. Shit challenges colonial discourses of civilization and development, while, simultaneously, the public lavatory embodies the disbelief in a new beginning that the country's transformation from Rhodesia to Zimbabwe is alleged to engender. This is exemplified in a paragraph where the narrator runs into the beer hall toilets to vomit,

> I got up hastily and, escaping into the toilet, just made it to the bowl where I was violently sick. As I came out, wiping my mouth with the back of my hand, I collided with two massive breasts that were straining angrily against a thin T-shirt upon which was written the legend ZIMBABWE. (19)

The association of vomiting, toilets, and the strikingly big breasts of Julia – the narrator's school time friend, also referred to as 'a beerhall doll,' 'nigger whore' (20), and 'the bitch' (25) – with the great Zimbabwe legend puts the nation-building process into a light that repudiates glorious, solemn tones. The grotesque, deviant, and excessive materiality of the female body becomes a vehicle of the meanings of colonization and decolonization,[22] Zimbabwe being represented by Julia's grotesque and merchandized sexuality. Rhodesia, on the other hand, finds its representation in a township woman who has 'stains of semen… dripping down her as she walked' (49). At one moment, the narrator refers to his fellow nationals as 'whores … eaten to the core by the syphilis of the white man's coming' (75). The prostitute figure simultaneously conveys the idea of colonial degradation and post-independence disillusionment, capturing hence the continuum of relations between these two supposedly opposing paradigms. Julia's grotesque sexuality stands for the excess and lack of proportion that, according to Mbembe, characterizes the political and social life of the postcolony.[23] It is as if the worn out and broken grotesque of Rhodesian township woman got intensified in the post-independence 'newness' of Julia's young, overwhelming, and heavily made-up embodied being. There is something dubious in this sudden transformation from the old to the new that suggests that the newness might not be as new as it pretends to be.

So, in 'House of Hunger,' the grotesque most frequently finds its articulation in the realm of sexuality which is very closely intertwined with violence. Indeed, in the novella, the public violence of colonialism translates into what is seen as private, gendered forms of violence. As for the corpses of the guerillas, there are similar kinds of public 'displays' with

[22] See Mary Russo, *The Female Grotesque: Risk, Excess and Modernity* (New York: Routledge, 1994).
[23] Mbembe, *On the Postcolony*, 102.

a strong emphasis on the sex-violence nexus. One of these displays takes place during the narrator's childhood years. There is a 'husband actually fucking – raping – his wife ... in the thick of the excited crowd' (50). In the face of this brutal sexual violence, the audience is less shocked than fascinated:

> When at last – the crowd licked its lips and swallowed – when at last he pulled his penis out of her raw thing and stuffed it back into his trousers, I think she seemed to move a finger, which made us all wonder how she could have survived such a determined assault. (50)

It is noteworthy, however, that these kinds of public 'screwing shows' do not only take place before an audience of random by-passers, but that the characters, mainly the narrator, become subjected to them within the intimacy of the private sphere, as well. Therefore, in 'House of Hunger,' the intimate is continuously violated and the private violently made public. The characters can, at any moment whatsoever, become victims of an aggression that reduces them to mere 'meat and stains.' Illustrative of this threat of violence that haunts the intimate is a depiction of a moment between the narrator and Immaculate. The narrator comes to see whether Immaculate is alright after being severely beaten by Peter. Their talk is interrupted by the sound of a heavy stone thrown on the roof, followed by the narrator's cat's carrion through the window, which conveys the idea of 'House of Hunger' as not-home and not-safe. Significantly, the allegedly private space of the home is also aggressed in the narrator's repeated exposure to the abusive sexuality of his family members. Here the narrator returns home from the beer hall to see Peter 'screwing' Immaculate 'underneath the table. Before I could retreat,' the narrator recalls, 'Peter said crossly, "Come in: sit down. This is home, man"' (27).

Eventually, Peter removes the blanket that covers them, exposing the narrator to the sight of their bodies in the middle of sex act. In the face of this intimidating sight, the narrator flees and gets drunk only to find himself later sleeping in the same bed with Immaculate. Occasional suggestions that the narrator is indeed involved with Immaculate put the two brothers' relationship into a somewhat incestuous light. This rather peculiar dynamism between the narrator, Peter, and Immaculate is not by any means a unique example of the grotesquely incestuous intimacies taking place within the narrator's family. There are several depictions of how the narrator, during his childhood years, becomes subjected to his parents', especially his mother's, vulgar sexuality. At four years of age, the narrator is kept awake at night by the 'maniacal symphonies' of his parents 'screwing' (48). When the father is away, an unknown man takes his place, with 'tremendous groans and grunts erupting from that bed' (48). Indeed, at one point, the mother is portrayed as a prostitute, 'a hard worker in screwing,' 'more feared than respected' (78). The mother imposes her vulgar sex education on her son:

> She would contemptuously give me a long sermon about how girls are 'easy' and 'why don't you get on with laying one or two?' Or three. Or four. Or five. 'There is nothing to it,' she said. 'You stick it in the hole between the water and the earth, it's easy. She splays out her legs and you bunch your pelvis between her thighs and Strike! right between her water and her earth. You strike like a fire and she'll take you and your balls all in … Why don't you get on with laying one and stop messing my sheets?' (78)

The mother's 'piece of advice' entails the sex-violence nexus so loudly articulated throughout the novella, also captured by the narrator's friend, Harry – 'Nigger girls are just meat' (13). The narrator's mother is not unique in her recourse to prostitution and in how she exposes the children to her merchandized sexuality. At school, the narrator had a friend whose mother had turned into a 'common drunken whore' (64) in order to afford her children's school fees, 'coaching' (61) also one of the narrator's school time friends into the profession. The narrator is growing up with the continuous presence of harsh sexual acts, often enacted by his closest relatives. 'The street education' (48), as the narrator calls it, also includes public masturbation shows performed by his own brother. Watching Peter masturbating before his audience, the narrator witnesses him 'losing control,' 'And, moaning like something out of this world, he came and came and came like new wine that cannot be contained within old cloth' (49). This grotesque image of his brother's body in the state of transformation remains imprinted on the narrator's mind, 'I swallowed thickly, but my mouth was dry. And my mouth, it seems, has been dry ever since' (49). After his childhood and youth experiences of grotesque sexuality, the narrator's reality continues to turn around violently grotesque sexual imagery, such as shooting sex films (68) and listening to prostitutes' accounts on their white clients' fetishisms with urination and excrement (51).

On the whole, in 'House of Hunger,' sexuality is stripped of all privacy; it is made public and it turns into violent, crudely material performances that, in their own abject logic, fascinate spectators. The low imagery of copulating bodies ridicules and imitates as much the noble colonial discourses of development and civilization as the solemnity of post-colonial nation-building narratives, which in fact continue the very legacy they are supposed to resist. In this sense, the bodies become material sites on which meanings write themselves and where the boundaries between the individual and the social are disturbed and transgressed. It must be emphasized that the embodied subjects themselves further represent and nourish the spirit of violence through their acts. This disturbs a reading of the violent, sexualized grotesque simply as a form of resistance to colonial and nationalist discourses. Indeed, as the narrator observes at one point, mental and physical diseases taking over the body are 'symptoms of a malign order' (7). Understanding the capacity of the 'malign order' to imprint itself on, and to be reproduced in, the private intimacy of the embodied subjectivity, the narrator goes on to sigh hopelessly in the face of his own degenerating mental health, 'How could I just get over it, for heaven's sake?' (7). On a more concrete level, there are several references to venereal diseases in the novella. What is noteworthy in this respect is that the diseases are never just private affairs. In the narrator's family, anti-VD sets are gifts from father to son and from brother to brother (3; 78). As such, sexuality is anything but the subject's personal concern, and so it enters into the realm of the grotesque.

So, Marechera writes the threat of violence as an unavoidable aspect of intimate relationships. Besides the crude sexually motivated violence defining the narrator's family life, his intimacy with women is also marked by the constant threat of getting physically assaulted. His relation with Patricia, a white woman, incites right-wing demonstrators to violence against the couple (72). The narrator is trying to protect the physically disabled Patricia against the group's assault, an attempt in which he obviously fails:

> They slammed into me, banged me where it hurt, and kept knocking me from every direction. I did not – must not – dare fall and cover my face with my hands; they would simply plough into me. I smacked them right back, buffeted them down, thumped them back, whacked them down, as they pummeled and pounded and battered into me. I kicked, booted, kneed, and cudgeled into them as they bulldozed into me and pile-drove me into one lump of pain. I clubbed, coshed, slugged, whipped, flogged and bashed into them as they sledge-hammered into me. (73)

The depiction of the attack is particularly interesting in that it displays bodies transgressing their physical boundaries and, through the act of violence, entering the realm of the other body. Indeed, it almost seems that the parties of the fight merge into one embodied, wounded entity; a somewhat particular vision of 'interracial' intimacy.

If, in the sexual context, bodies – women's bodies in particular

– are reduced to mere meat, then in the case of physical violence, they risk becoming just 'stains.' The narrator, for instance, is beaten into stains by his father, mother, and brother respectively. When the narrator is nine years old, his father violently pushes him against the wall, making him fall 'back into [his] corner onto the exercise-books. Staining them with blood' (14). Later on, his brother calls him 'bookshit' (4), spits on him, and hits his head against the wall, with children cheering outside, 'Break its neck' (5). His mother, too, hits him when he talks to her in English. These cases exemplify the perplexities related to the colonial education and 'civilization' as simultaneously elevating and suppressive. The narrator's body embodies these contradictory meanings and becomes the subject of his family's aggressions. In 'House of Hunger,' close relationships expose embodied subjects to the omnipresent risk of violence instead of providing them security and protection. There is, for instance, the narrator's friend Nestar who lets her son be beaten up by the narrator and his friends. Uniquely annoyed by the fact that the beating might dirty her decoration she says, 'Not in here, if you please. The basement is the best place' (55). The acts of violence that occur between Nestar's son and the narrator and his friend are illustrative of the overwhelming spirit of violence and the ways in which violence cumulates – Nestar's son beats and rapes the sister of the narrator's friend, who, in turn, avenges his sister only to be beaten up later by the friends of Nestar's son. The beating is depicted in detail, with the narrator's dentures cracking, him 'trying to spit out the fragments' (75). As the narrator states, 'he thrashed me so much I blacked out, speechless' (76). The violence tears the body into separate fragments that cannot hold together. When the narrator comes to, he finds himself on a street knocking on a door and entering as no-one answers. The house is deserted and the narrator's physical pain merges with psychological malaise, 'I began to wonder if *I* was really in there; perhaps I was a mere creation of the rooms themselves' (76). Ultimately, the narrator flees 'from the house like a madman who has seen the inside of his own ravings' (77). This scene is illustrative of what Jane Bryce has analyzed as 'the ease of transition between inner and outer'[24] in Marechera's work, here occurring as the seizure of the inner by an external condition. After his escape from the house, the narrator manages to get to a hospital where his head is X-rayed. The sight of the X-rays is an uneasy experience that leaves its imprint on the narrator, 'There was nothing to my mind, to my head, but a skull that had some grinning teeth missing. That broken grin, I have never been able to erase it out of my mind' (77). The mocking smile of the skull reminds the narrator of his inescapable materiality and the inevitability of death that his embodied being constantly carries within. Further, as it is suggested in another context, the raw materiality of the body is particularly interesting as it is seen to reveal fundamental aspects of identity and also that subjects *are* their bodies. 'That's what being human means. Insides. Entrails,' Julia says. She continues, 'I wanted to look at my insides. Rip them insides out and see what I really was' (46).

Marechera's grotesque 'meat and stain' philosophy can be read as a challenge to both colonial civilization discourses and anti-colonial nationalism. What should be emphasized, however, is that, as Mbembe maintains, by engaging in the grotesque imagery, the embodied postcolonial subject internalizes the aesthetics of vulgarity of the *commandement*.[25] In this sense, the critical power of the grotesque is profoundly ambiguous. In a similar vein, Esty suggests that the grotesque imagery complicates 'moral and political binaries by diffusing guilt and shame,'[26] which implies that instead of constructing utopias and believing in revolution, 'the excremental satirist bears witness to the conversion of his society's political energies

---

[24] Bryce, 'Inside/out,' 222.
[25] Mbembe, *On the Postcolony*, 128.
[26] Esty, 'Excremental Postcolonialism,' 34.

– and his own aesthetic efforts – into shit.'[27] Indeed, Esty's reading challenges interpretations of the grotesque as purely counter-discursive and emphasizes postcolonial intellectuals' inevitable involvement with the power structures that they are attacking. This complicity is also acknowledged by Marechera, whose nameless narrator's – Marechera's own writer alter ego – reaction to his friend's comment after a short literary discussion is illustrative:

> 'You literary chaps are our only hope,' Harry began.
>
> I choked politely on my drink. Then we are sunk, I thought.
>
> I began to feel like those stale mornings when the cold wind writhes about purposelessly as if there was nothing but air in the gleaming casket of creation. The sick juices were welling up in me, making me want to vomit. And that blasted barman was still staring with great interest into my face. (16)

Contrasting hopes with the writer-figure's 'sick juices' and his sudden urge to vomit suggests that the potentials of postcolonial writerly dissidence and resistance remain highly ambivalent.

In 'House of Hunger,' the (post-)colonial condition writes itself on the materiality of the allegedly private intimacy of the body. This entails that the body operates with the world in a two-way manner – the world enters the body through acts that break down boundaries of enclosure; and, vice versa, the body connects to the world through the continuous escape of all kinds of bodily fluids, as well as acts of sex and violence which both prove to be essentially boundary-crossing acts. The grotesque in 'House of Hunger' most often manifests itself in sexual and violent acts, although the novel makes use of secretion imagery as well. While Marechera's grotesque could be read as a Bakhtinian counter-discursive practice ridiculing both colonialist and post-independence discourses of development, it must be acknowledged that by engaging in

[27] Ibid., 44.

the grotesquely violent aesthetics, postcolonial subjects also participate in *representing* the sexualized and racialized logic of the very discourses they are supposed to oppose. Moreover, 'House of Hunger' articulates the tension between hopes and disillusionment that is constructed in a gender-specific manner. Male figures yearn for lost heroes only to realize the futility of their aspirations; female characters give voice to a hope for an elsewhere that reaches beyond nostalgia for something irretrievably lost. Women's aspirations are silenced and their bodies reduced to mere meat through sexualized violence. The Marecheran grotesque seems to escape redemptive readings and to put emphasis on the disillusioned condition of postcolonial complicity.

4 Tracing the Stain in Marechera's 'House of Hunger'

GRANT HAMILTON

Dambudzo Marechera's *The House of Hunger*[1] is a text that has drawn widely divergent critical responses. As Drew Shaw makes clear in his essay 'Transgressing Traditional Narrative Form,' those critics who supported the official literary aesthetic of social realism in the newly independent Zimbabwe found much to be concerned about in Marechera's writing.[2] Mbulelo Mzamane, Musaemura Zimunya and Juliet Okonkwo gave something less than a glowing recommendation of Marechera's experimental writing and in his book, *Those Years of Drought: The Birth of Black Zimbabwean Literature in English*, Zimunya derides the fractured nature of Marechera's writing, reducing it to nothing more than an 'eclectic babble' which cannot 'enrich one's own culture.'[3] Evidencing this, Zimunya singles out the ending of 'House of Hunger' because he can see 'no technical link between the last fragment of the novella … and the rest of the story.'[4] In a similar spirit, Okonkwo writes in her review of *The House of Hunger* that Marechera's writing is 'deliberately … sordid and shocking.'[5] She goes on to write, his 'excessive interest in sex activity, his tireless attempt to rake up filth, his insistent expression of a debased philosophy built around

---

[1] Dambudzo Marechera, *The House of Hunger* (1978; London: Penguin, 2002). Unless otherwise indicated, further page references are in the main text.

[2] Drew Shaw, 'Transgressing Traditional Narrative Form,' in *Emerging Perspectives on Dambudzo Marechera*, eds Flora Veit-Wild and Anthony Chennells (Trenton, NJ: Africa World Press, 1999), 3-22.

[3] Musaemura Zimunya, *Those Years of Drought and Hunger: The Birth of Black Zimbabwean Literature in English* (Gweru: Mambo Press, 1982), 128.

[4] Ibid., 118.

[5] Juliet Okonkwo, 'A Review of *The House of Hunger*,' *Okike: An African Journal of New Writing* (June 1981), 91.

"stains on a sheet"' is 'alien to Africa – a continent of hope and realizable dreams.'[6] Importantly, these critics dismiss the value of Marechera's writing because it seems to consciously position itself outside of Emmanuel Ngara and Fay Chung's influential vision of Zimbabwean literature as something that can 'play a truly positive and constructive role in the building of socialism in Zimbabwe.'[7] According to these critics then, the 'decadent avant-garde European attitude and style'[8] of Marechera's writing means that he has little, if anything, to add to the political discourse of revitalization circulating the newly independent nation of Zimbabwe.

However, it is the contention of this paper that Marechera's 'House of Hunger' has something extremely valuable to add to the political discourse of Zimbabwe. Far from this experimental piece of writing signaling Marechera's ever-increasing distance from the concerns of Zimbabwe and her people, 'House of Hunger' ultimately offers a way in which the people of Zimbabwe can begin to productively rethink the very idea of nation. And this process begins with recognizing the significance of the stain.

So, Okonkwo is right to draw attention to Marechera's *ritournelle* of the stain. However, it is more important to the political condition of Marechera's writing than she is willing, or able, to recognize. While the stain might be alien to Okonkwo's vision of a continent of 'hope and realizable dreams,' it is absolutely central to Marechera's political vision of the ontological and epistemological landscape of the Zimbabwean people. For Marechera, the stain is unpleasant – it is not something to be rejoiced in; it is not something to be celebrated. Nonetheless, it defines the very limits of life. After all, Marechera shows in 'House of Hunger' that we emerge from the promise of a stain,

---

[6] Ibid., 91.
[7] Emmanuel Ngara and Fay Chung, *Socialism, Education and Development: A Challenge to Zimbabwe* (Harare: Zimbabwe Publishing House, 1985), 116.
[8] Okonkwo, 'A Review,' 91.

and it is, as the death of the narrator's father testifies, to the stain that we will return. But, this only hints at its value. Importantly, the stain stands as the material fact of the Derridean 'trace.' Found scattered throughout Jacques Derrida's work, the trace is perhaps most easy to understand as a trajectory that marks 'the absence of a presence, an always already absent present.'[9] That is to say, the trace announces a certain kind of lack, a vacuity, an emptiness. It exposes the fact that something has disappeared; that something no longer persists where it once did even though the evidence of its presence remains to be read by an other.[10] This is the significance of the stain; it announces the absence of presence – an absent present. And, this, I want to argue, is how Marechera sees and renders Zimbabwe in 'House of Hunger.' Marechera sees the absence of presence everywhere, especially in the social and political life of Zimbabwe. Such absence, then, leads him to characterize Zimbabwe and the drives of the Zimbabwean people through the most visceral experience of absence – hunger. Zimbabwe, like the narrator's own psychology, is a House of Hunger.

Marechera, though, is not content to simply expose the absence that seemingly describes the contours of Zimbabwe and its people. His overwhelming rendition of Zimbabwe might be, as Grant Lilford notes, 'a dry blighted landscape which reflects the drought in people's souls,'[11] but he also suggests a means for escaping the condition of this profound thirst or hunger. Written at the same time that guerilla fighters under the command of Robert Mugabe and Joshua Nkomo

---

[9] Gayatri Chakravorty Spivak, introduction to *Of Grammatology*, by Jacques Derrida, trans. Gayatri Chakravorty Spivak (Baltimore: The Johns Hopkins UP, 1974), xviii.

[10] Of course, I am simplifying Derrida's account of the trace, here. The merest hint of the further complexity of the term is given when Derrida writes, 'The trace is not only the disappearance of origin... according to the path that we follow it means that the origin did not even disappear, that it was never constituted except reciprocally by a non-origin, the trace, which thus becomes the origin of the origin.' *Of Grammatology*, 61.

[11] Grant Lilford, 'Traces of Tradition: The Probability of the Marecheran Manfish,' in *Emerging Perspectives on Dambudzo Marechera*, 283.

had forced Ian Smith's white minority government to make a series of conciliatory gestures,[12] 'House of Hunger' recognizes the curious psychological and spiritual torpor sweeping across Zimbabwe. Indeed, it is peculiar that at the moment when the revolutionary nationalists of the Zimbabwe African National Union (ZANU) and Zimbabwe African People's Union (ZAPU) should be enjoying the rapture of standing on the threshold of political self-determination, Marechera apprehends a sense of absence, or a profound exhaustion, in the common sensibility of the Zimbabwean people. For Marechera, it is the product of the recognition that it is perhaps too easy to blame the 'capitalists and imperialists' and 'the bloody whites' (9) for the condition in which Zimbabwe finds itself. It is also, perhaps, too easy to organize and administer independent Zimbabwe without considering what shape, what dimensions, the new nation should take. In the rush to fill the void of Smith's departing neo-colonial administration, Marechera sees only the inevitable failure of the new state and the promise of further conflict – a nation built on 'hate' (17). Zimbabweans, Marechera seems to caution, should not be too quick to simply assume the structures and systems of the outgoing neo-colonial regime; they should take hold of this moment of the interregnum, the moment between administrations, to rethink the very idea of nation.

Significantly, the most productive way of interrogating the idea of the nation, Marechera suggests, is by thinking through the concept anew. It is a process that French poststructuralist philosopher Gilles Deleuze terms 'outside thought.'[13] The claim that is made is that only by looking to fresh, unique ideas

---

[12] See Eliakim Sibanda, *The Zimbabwe African People's Union 1961–87: A Political History of Insurgency in Southern Rhodesia* (Trenton, NJ: Africa World Press, 2005).

[13] Deleuze's discussion of 'outside thought' or 'nomad thought' is scattered throughout his writing. However, his most concentrated discussion of this kind of thought is to be found in Gilles Deleuze and Félix Guattari, '1227: Treatise on Nomadology: – The War Machine,' in *A Thousand Plateaus: Capitalism and Schizophrenia vol. 2*, trans. Brian Massumi (London: Athlone, 1988), 351-423.

that emanate from beyond Zimbabwe, beyond all formalized discourses on nations and nationalism, beyond the confines of the House of Hunger, can the soon-to-be independent nation of Zimbabwe become 'Zimbabwe' – a new independent territory of the people – rather than a mere shadowy repetition of Rhodesia. Marechera sets out the program for doing so at the end of the novella through the voice of the narrator's estranged father, who tells stories that are 'oblique, rambling, and fragmentary' (79). As such, far from there being 'no technical link between the last fragment of the novella … and the rest of the story' as claimed by Zimunya, the ending of the novella is revealed to be not only vital to the structure of 'House of Hunger,' but also absolutely vital to understanding Marechera's political vision for the future of Zimbabwe.

To understand Marechera's political vision of Zimbabwe, then, is to understand the way in which he thinks of the stain. In 'House of Hunger,' the stain is written into every part of life and across the world. From the stains on a bed sheet that hold the promise of a new life, to the bloodstains on a plate that show a hunger has been satiated and a life has been sustained, to the stains of God that are visible in the sky (41-2), Marechera shows that it is the stain that best shows the value and significance of life because of the traces of other presences that emerge from it. For the narrator, stains are the material evidence of the emotions that course through humanity. Somewhat poetically, he proclaims, 'Love or even hate or the desire for revenge are just so many stains on a sheet, on a wall, on a page even. This page' (55). But, since the stain is intimately related to the trace of these other presences, it is clear that it must signify more than its own material presence. Indeed, the stain signifies the infinite complexity of life – the intimate and unexpected relationships that can evolve between objects and events, the past and the present, the actual and the virtual. As such, the stain can be thought of as something like a sign or an emblem. That is to say, the meaning of a stain is not to be found in its material presence but rather somewhere along the trajectory of the traces which are produced by the observer's encounter with it. Such traces seem to send the observer barreling into the past. And, this indeed appears to be the case as the narrator dives into the past in order to explain the bloodstains that appear on his school books. He recalls:

> I remember coming home one day. Running with glee. I forget what I was happy about ... I burst into the room and all at once exploded into my story, telling it restlessly and with expansive gestures, telling it to mother who was staring. A stinging slap that made my ear sing stopped me. I stared up at mother in confusion. She hit me again. 'How dare you speak in English to me,' she said crossly. 'You know I don't understand it, and if you think because you're educated...' (13)

After destroying his English exercise books in a fit of rage and fleeing his mother, he returns home later with new exercise books. His father sits quietly eating his dinner:

> A chair, drawn back, creaked. I tensed. I stared stonily at the floor, at the books. The blow knocked my front teeth out ... He pushed me and I fell back into my corner onto the exercise books. Staining them with blood. I was nine years old then. (14)

Now, although it seems as though the narrator descends into the past in order to explain the bloodstains on his exercise books, here, what is actually happening is something quite different. In fact, the narrator is 'pulling' the past into the present. For example, it is important to realize that this recollection does more than simply explain the bloodstains on his books; it explains the *significance* of the bloodstains on his books, and in so doing brings the past to bear on the present. The significance of the bloodstains is not that they signify the terrible physical violence that the narrator endures in the family home, but rather that they announce the moment when the narrator learns of the incendiary nature of language. It is, after all, his unthinking use of English that sparks this violent episode. From this point on, the narrator regards language as a kind of combat. It can cause people to erupt suddenly in fits of anger and rage (25-6); it is a powerful force that must be marshaled in the right way. Yet, as the narrator soon discovers, it is not so easy to bring a combative language under control. He explains:

> English is my second language, Shona my first. When I talked it was in the form of an interminable argument, one side of which was always expressed in English and the other side always in Shona ... I felt gagged by this absurd contest between Shona and English. I knew no other language: my French and Latin were enough to make me wary of conversing in them. However, some nights I could feel the French and the Latin fighting it out in the shadowy background of the English and Shona. The fights completely muzzled me. (30)

The narrator's violent introduction to the forcefulness of language is doubled by the experience of languages entering into combat with each other, which again leaves him the victim. As the battle for supremacy rages in his mind, the narrator is left 'feeling literally robbed of words' (30). However, it is from episodes such as this that the psychological landscape of the narrator begins to emerge. That is to say, the narrator begins to be understood as the product of the past being brought to bear on the present. He becomes the stain of a life lived.

So, the trace brings the past to bear on the present. It is a simple formulation, but one that is absolutely vital to understanding Marechera's political vision of Zimbabwe. Actually, it is the fact that the past is *continuously* being pulled into, or onto, the present that is essential to understanding Marechera's political vision of Zimbabwe. One of the more important effects of this insatiable movement is that there is, in effect, little room left for the present to exist. As more and more of the past is pulled onto the present, it begins to totalize discursive space. Indeed, what can be said of the present, it seems, must first have been said of the past. So, the past begins to dominate the present by occupying the sites of both the singular and the specific.[14] For example, this is exactly the way in which the narrator conceptualizes the impoverished ontological condition of his generation. In conversation with his old school friend and co-revolutionary, Julia, the narrator turns to history. After explaining how King Lobengula was tricked by Charles Rudd into signing away the mineral rights to Matabeleland, he continues:

> I don't like to blame him though, for making us all like this. Of course he was silly, poking his head into a Pandora's Box … Chief Moghabi refused to submit to authority and was killed. Chief Ngomo did the same and he and his people were killed … Lobengula fled Bulawayo. And after crossing the Shangani admitted defeat … The one thing that bugs me about the man is that he even loved white men. That he killed my people like cattle, the way Germans killed Jews. And he loved white men … is this all there is to our history? There is a stinking deceit at the heart of it. Petty intrigues … and so here we are all sticky with the stinking stains of history. (42-3)

The narrator's suspicion is that this potted history is all that one needs to understand the singular condition of the Zimbabwean people. What can be said of the past, which as the narrator insists in this instance is reducible to nothing more than the 'petty intrigues' of a select few, tells us about the condition of the present. For the narrator, the people of his generation are nothing more than the stain of this inglorious history – merely the progeny of Lobengula's almost autoscopic self-deception and his nation's deceitful suitor. It may be no

---

[14] The notion of the singular and the specific is taken from the work of Gilles Deleuze and discussed at length in Peter Hallward, *Absolutely Postcolonial: Writing Between the Singular and the Specific* (Manchester: Manchester UP, 2001).

surprise that the narrator's generation has inherited this genetic characteristic of deceit. However, it is some surprise to the narrator that he sees it at work in his own actions. Describing the moment he chose 'to become a man,' the narrator shows how willing he is to deceive himself:

> I had got over aching for the unobtainable Julia who had been left in my charge by my best friend. I was at that point where it's no use fussing and fretting whether one could with a will find some money and dare the unknown terrors of VD – with a little help from dagga. I braved it one stormy night and survived to regret it … The experience left me marked by an irreverent disgust for women which has never left me. Never again would I suffer wholeheartedly for any woman. (3)

To 'dare the unknown terrors of VD' and convince yourself that it will not in some way leave its mark is perhaps the narrator's most ill-considered effort of self-deception. Clearly the experience does mark him. After all, he is left with 'an irreverent disgust for women' – an indelible, psychological stain that will forever draw the experience of venereal disease into his perception of the world. But, from this episode, we see again the way in which the past asserts itself on the present in the form of the stain.

As these assertions of the past proliferate in the present, the significance or meaning of the contemporary world finds itself being gradually replaced. That is to say, what is found meaningful in the present is never anything more than a product of the past. This is why the only thing that the narrator finds significant in contemporary Zimbabwe is the stain. The stain announces the trace, and the trace determines the significance of what *is* by bringing it into association with what *was* – by pulling the past onto the present. The result of this movement is that the past invades the present by closing off, or exhausting, the very possibility of the present. As such, the stain is always the sign of completion – of a life *lived*, rather than a life *being* lived. For example, consider the way in which the narrator understands his father's death:

> The old man died beneath the wheels of the twentieth century. There was nothing left but stains, bloodstains and fragments of flesh, when the whole length of it was through with eating him. And the same thing is happening to my generation ... The bulldozers have been and gone and where once our heroes danced there is nothing but a hideous stain. (45)

Here the narrator recognizes that the present seems to be no more than the conclusion of other events. So, while again rendering the dynamic of the singular and specific by bringing the sense of his father's specific death into relation with the blighted existential condition of his own generation, the narrator shows that the stain is the sign of both a life lived and a generation that has existed before it has even been born. This, then, exposes the framework of the profound exhaustion that lies at the heart of the Zimbabwean people. It is an exhaustion that finds articulation in the conspicuously repeated phrase 'what else is there?' (12). This, in fact, is how the township's noted photographer, Solomon, responds to the narrator's questions about his penchant for sleeping with white women. We are told that Solomon's

> arm swept the panorama of barbed wire, whitewashed houses, drunks, prostitutes, the angelic choirs of god-created flies, and the dust that erupted in to little clouds of divine grace wherever the golden sunlight deigned to strike. His god-like gesture stopped abruptly – pointing straight at the stinking public lavatory. 'What else is there, man?' he repeated. I think I saw his point. (11-12)

The 'point' is that the township – which is rendered as a metonym of Zimbabwe – has nothing to offer. It exists in a ruined condition. The barbed wire signifies an endemic sense of mistrust; drunks and prostitutes suggest a certain kind of desperation; the disjunctive synthesis of angelic choirs and the hum of flies hints at a spiritual void; and the clouds of dust that are illuminated by the sunlight imply a dry, bleached, infertile landscape. It is, then, no accident that Solomon concludes his 'god-like gesture' at the public lavatory, a place reserved solely for the basest of human functions. For Solomon, the only thing to do is escape the township, turn away from its people, and go elsewhere in order to finally live.

For Immaculate, who is perhaps dearest to the narrator's heart, the absolute opposite is true. The township in which she and the narrator live is everything; there can be nothing else:

> She and I had gone down the valley and crossed the river and walked up the ancient stone tracks that led up to the old fortifications which our warlike ancestors had used in time of war. The soft skin stretched effortlessly over the pain behind her delicate oval face. We were looking down over the valley, down upon the township in which we lived. 'What else is there?' she repeated. (12)

As such, the sense of her response to the township rushes in the absolute opposite direction to that described by Solomon. In spite of everything, Immaculate holds on to the idea that there is nothing more important than the township. In this way, then, it defines the territory of her existence. But in this, the narrator detects more than a hint of romanticism. And, no matter how much he would like to succumb to her vision, he simply cannot. He writes, 'She made me want to dream, made me believe in visions, in hope. But the rock and grit of the earth denied this' (12). For the narrator, the true condition of the township is born from the marriage of Solomon's visceral vision of reality and Immaculate's romantic vision. The township is, at the same time, everything and nothing. Or, put another way, the township demonstrates that everything is nothing, and that nothing is everywhere. The two visions come together, therefore, to highlight the inescapable nature of the profound absence that determines the ontological and epistemological condition of the people.

Escape from the pervasive sense of exhaustion that characterizes this profound feeling of an absent present cannot even be relocated in the promise, or possibility, of the future. Early on in the novella, the narrator explains how the excitement of the promise of political self-determination soon evaporated from the people. He writes that there was

> an excitement of the spirit which made us all wander about in search of the unattainable elixir which our restlessness presaged. But the search was doomed from the start because the elixir seemed to be right under our noses and yet not really there. The freedom we craved for … was so alive in our breath and in our fingers that one became intoxicated by it even before one had actually found it … This was the paradox whose discovery left us uneasy, sly and at best with the ache of knowing that one would never feel that way again … the emptiness was deep-seated in the gut. We knew that before us lay another vast emptiness whose appetite for things living was at best wolfish. Life stretched out like a series of hunger-scoured hovels stretching endlessly towards the horizon. (3)

Just as the past is pulled onto the present in order to offer some kind of significance in the contemporary world, the future is similarly reined in. The narrator explains how the promise of the future is lived in the present without it first being secured. He characterizes it as

> the way a man licks his lips in his dream of a feast; the way a woman dances in her dream of a carnival; the way the old man ran like a gazelle in his yearning for the funeral games of his youth. (3)

The freedom promised by the revolutionary Zimbabwe African National Union – Patriotic Front (ZANU-PF) is felt and rehearsed by the people of Zimbabwe, but, importantly, never experienced. The spirit of the time might be understood as the joy of standing on the immediate brink of political self-determination, but for the narrator it remains a spectral presence. There never comes a moment in which this promise, this yearning for a democratic political voice, comes into being. Rather, as Brian Raftopoulos makes clear, 'the new government under President Mugabe became increasingly repressive, seeking to force opposition either into alliance with ZANU, or into silence.'[15] Of course, the result of such political maneuvers was not the freedom of a people who had been oppressed and marginalized under Ian Smith's premiership, but rather the development of a 'formal one-party presidentialist state.'[16] As such, the promise of freedom slowly falls away from the people. As Mugabe installs himself as head of state, the future quickly becomes a repetition of old forms, leaving nothing but the promise of 'another vast emptiness' before the people. The utopian dreaming of the people, then, is exposed for what it is – the promise of an absence; a literal *eu-topos*.

In this way, the future in Marechera's 'House of Hunger' takes on the character of the future outlined by Derrida in *Of Grammatology*. He writes that 'the future can only be anticipated in the form of an absolute danger. It is that which breaks absolutely with constituted normality and can only be proclaimed, presented, as a sort of monstrosity.'[17] The monstrousness of the narrator's vision of the future is that it is only understandable as another kind of absence. As such, it works against the production of the 'new.' If the future is absent then nothing can change – nothing can become anything else. That is to say, the very possibility of organizing yourself or a society in a new way collapses. Indeed, the future collapses back onto the present along with the promise of liberation. From this

---

[15] Brian Raftopoulos, 'Beyond the House of Hunger: Democratic Struggle in Zimbabwe,' *Review of African Political Economy* 20, no. 55 (November 1992), 57.

[16] Ibid., 57.

[17] Derrida, *Of Grammatology*, 5.

state of affairs, society descends into a chronic exhaustion. In short, the future no longer offers any possibility for development and so people begin to simply exist, or survive, in the contemporary world. Yet, as the narrator is acutely aware, the problem is that the present has been usurped by the past. Caught in the feedback loop of a future that has collapsed back onto the present, which has always-already been usurped by the past, the people of Zimbabwe are cast into the experience a profound torpor.

Therefore, for the narrator, the present is doubly impoverished. First, it is merely the stain of the petty intrigues of history; and second, it is merely the stain of a failed future. The inevitable conclusion that the narrator makes is that the present shows nothing more than an absence of presence; it is merely the trace of the past and future. And, because of this, the present assumes a ghostly, shadowy, quality. Derrida is quick to note that 'the trace is *nothing*, it is not an entity.'[18] Similarly, he writes in *Speech and Phenomena* that 'the trace has, properly speaking, no place.'[19] This, then, is the condition of the present as understood by the narrator – it exists in a curious state of non-being. As such, the fact of the material presence of the present only compounds the feeling that some essential vitality has been leeched away. This is why the narrator thinks of himself as 'a dead tree, dry of branch and decayed at the roots' (19). He is undoubtedly a physical presence in the world, but the energy that describes a life has simply evaporated. Under such conditions, physical presence only serves to announce the loss of the dynamic quality of the world. And so, the narrator thinks of it as something to be scorned. He writes, 'I found the idea of humanity, the concept of mankind, more attractive than actual beings. On a baser level I could not forgive man, myself, for being utterly and crudely *there*' (7). Again, physical

---

[18] Ibid., 75.

[19] Jacques Derrida, *Speech and Phenomena: And Other Essays on Husserl's Theory of Signs*, trans. David B. Allison (Evanston, IL: Northwestern UP, 1973), 156.

presence only reminds the narrator of the essential qualities that are missing from the world. The world itself, understood as a stain, is inert, vacuous, and total in the sense that it seems to be inescapable. As Philip makes clear to the narrator, there seems to be no way out of this condition of absence. Talking of the various attempts of the people to assert their physical presence on the world, Philip sagely observes that 'there's a lot of anger gets you nowhere. There's heaps of consideration gets you nowhere too. It's just tickets to nowhere, everything is' (59). In this way, the totalizing stance of absence necessarily forms the walls of reality. Given that neither history nor the future can offer any respite or remedy to the overwhelming sense of exhaustion that emerges from this condition of the absent present, it seems that all avenues of escape – of appeal to a better future – are lost. So, talking to the narrator, Philip says:

> There's hungry people out there. There's homeless people out there. There's many going about in the rags of their birthday suit. And they's all mad. They's all got designs. You've got designs. I've got designs. But we're all designing in a sea full of shit. (59)

What Philip describes here is the way in which all thought seems to be determined by a core reality. For Gilles Deleuze, it is the reality derived from a pattern of cognitive conformity that comes 'from the State apparatus, and which defines for it goals and paths, conduits, channels, organs, an entire *organon*.'[20] In short, such State-thought overwhelms the capacity for individual thought. It insists on a very particular kind of truth and 'true thinking' – one that lends gravity to the State by announcing a *cogitatio universalis*.[21] In so doing, State-thought limits the possibility of original thinking and thereby also the composition of reality. The reality determined by such State-thought, therefore, is one drawn from a past

---

[20] Deleuze and Guattari, *A Thousand Plateaus*, 374.
[21] Ibid., 376.

that consumes the present and a future that only exposes the impossibility of change. This arrangement may 'guarantee' the duration of the State, but it also means that people are locked into a type of living and thinking that can do nothing to change the condition of life. Without imagination, indeed, without the ability to think of a 'beyond' to State-thought, the people of Zimbabwe enter into a condition of terminal repetition – an inescapable exhaustion.

Yet, the novella begins, 'I got my things and left' (1). At the very least, the narrator recognizes the need to try and escape the 'inescapable.' Physically, the narrator gets no further than the township's beerhall; but conceptually, he manages to transcend the exhaustion of State-thought in order to posit the way in which Zimbabwe might begin its radical recovery. After the tirade of violent histories and collapsed futures that stride across his mind as he sits in the beerhall, the narrator's final thoughts settle on the memory of a set of discontinuous, fractured narratives told to him by his father. It is these tales that allow the narrator to understand better the condition of absence, and ultimately begin to unlock the condition of exhaustion, that he sees in Zimbabwean life.

The first tale the narrator's father tells is of a man's desire to slake 'an unknown hunger' (79). It is a hunger that has driven the man 'from himself, from his friends, from his family, from the things of his first world' (79). We are told that he wandered 'alone and bareheaded under the sun' (79-80). The invitation to read this 'man' as the narrator, then, is clearly made since nothing describes the narrator's relationship to himself and, indeed, others, better than this. The narrator's father continues:

> He fed on his discontent; but it did not fill up his belly. He fed on his hatred of all things; but that did not quench his thirst. And then he fed on dreams, all kinds of vengeance, of forgiveness, of self-mutilation, of the love that is in all things. But even that did not quench his thirst, neither did it fill his hunger. (79)

But this does not only describe the narrator. This is a description of the singular and specific condition of the Zimbabwean people. As such, it finds a fundamental resonance with Philip's earlier observations on the inability of Zimbabweans to understand and think their way out of their condition of exhaustion. What is outlined, here, is the fact that all possible attempts to satiate the metaphysical hunger of the Zimbabwean nation – whether to satisfy it through taking hold of negative states or, indeed, the more productive states of forgiveness and love – are predestined to fail if the terms of such remedies are drawn from an already-existing condition. Importantly, this observation on hunger recognizes that the hunger itself is a product of this singular and specific environment, and so it cannot be satiated by returning to elements from within the same environment. The implication is that one must turn to the outside in order to productively rethink the condition of the contemporary world. Here, then, is the territory of the man's epiphany, 'As he listened to himself, to the thirst and to the hunger, he suddenly said in words of gold: "I will live at the head of the stream where all of man's questions begin"' (80). What the man realizes is that absence, hunger, cannot be fought into surrender. It cannot be fed in the hope that its appetite will be quieted. Since such hunger is everything and everywhere, the only hope of combating it is by first listening to what it means. Put simply, the man – who we might as well regard as the novella's narrator – finally comprehends that the only way to satiate this kind of totalizing hunger is first to understand the condition of absence and exhaustion that characterizes the ontological and epistemological condition of the people of Zimbabwe. To 'listen' to the significance of the absence in contemporary Zimbabwe is to realize that new questions about the possibility of life have to be asked. Such questions emerge from 'the head of the stream' that eventually becomes the territory of State-thought. That is to say, they emerge from beyond the *cogitatio universalis* of State-thought.

Such questions are, then, the product of what Deleuze calls 'outside thought.'[22]

Outside thought is above all else a counter-thought. It works in distinction to State-thought. Where State-thought sets up a universal method by appealing to the two sites of universality, imperium and republic, Deleuze explains that outside thought 'rejects this image and does things differently.'[23] Since it is outside of State-thought, such thinking does not inherit its form or trajectory from known ways of thinking. Rather, it is the product of 'something more distant than any external world... [and] something closer than any inner world.'[24] That is to say, it is a force of the specific, the 'private thinker,' and it inhabits a curious super-position that ultimately results in liberating thinking from the terrain of the already-said. To connect to the outside is not to delve into the past or even imagine the future; it is to release thought from the confinement of what *must* be thought in order to let it explore what *can* be thought. This, then, is the significance of the final tale told by the narrator's father. Invoking a sense of the magical, the father tells the story of a man who meets a green dwarf on his way home:

> 'Why do you walk with a crutch?' the dwarf asked with contempt ... 'Can't you see I have no crutch? Indeed, I have no use for it.' 'You have the biggest crutch I have ever seen a cripple use.' The man, astonished, and perhaps a little angry, demanded: 'What crutch?' And the dwarf, spitting again at the skulking chameleon, said: 'Why, your mind.' (82)

Here, then, is the key to unlocking the condition of exhaustion that afflicts the people of Zimbabwe. One must forgo what

---

[22] Deleuze comes to the term 'outside thought' through Michel Foucault's discussion of Maurice Blanchot's work. See Foucault's 'La pensée du dehors' in *Foucault/Blanchot: Maurice Blanchot: The Thought from Outside and Michel Foucault as I Imagine Him*, ed. and trans. Jeffrey Mehlman and Brian Massumi (New York: Zone Books, 1987).

[23] Deleuze and Guattari, *A Thousand Plateaus*, 379.

[24] Gilles Deleuze, *Negotiations, 1972–1990*, trans. Martin Joughin (New York: Columbia UP, 1995), 110.

is already-said, what is already-understood, in order to learn and see again the significance of the contemporary world. Only in this way can history recede from the shores of the present back into the past, and a vision of the future be revitalized. Only in this way can the significance of the present be restored. As the narrator's father realizes at the close of the novella, this turn to the outside may be a painful transition; it will certainly attract the attention of the Security State. But, outside thought once again promises a future to the people of Zimbabwe. In striking the crutches of State-thought from people's minds, it promises to remove the most profound stains of the nation.

5 Menippean Marechera

BILL ASHCROFT

Everybody agrees that Dambudzo Marechera is a unique, and uniquely difficult, figure in African literature. There is possibly no writer whose fiction is more enmeshed with his life, no writer whose life seems more like a picaresque novel. Commentary on his work has been sometimes almost obsessed with the ways in which his life intervenes in his writing, no doubt helped by the dominance of the narrating 'I.' In passages on language, nation, literary identity, sexuality and many others, the writer seems to be speaking from his own life. In many places the narrator's commentary is directly auto-biographical.[1] Yet, as Flora Veit-Wild says, 'Marechera was constantly re-inventing his biography,'[2] re-inventions that formed an apparently indispensable pre-text but no less fictional than his writing. Marechera's life was as rebellious as his work and this has inevitably acted as a magnet to commentary on the writing, 'a unique expression of self and postcolonial identity in contemporary African literature.'[3] A true ex-centric individual, he eschewed nation, language, education, career. He turned his back on the life of an educated African writer, and while offering blistering attacks on the Rhodesian regime he offered equally scathing critique of the newly independent national administration of Zimbabwe. The habitual linking of Marechera's subjectivity with his writing is no doubt enhanced

---

[1] See Dambudzo Marechera, *The Black Insider*, ed. Flora Veit-Wild (Trenton, N.J: Africa World Press, 1992), 30.

[2] Flora Veit-Wild, *Dambudzo Marechera: A Source Book on his Life and Work* (London: Hans Zell, 1992), xiii.

[3] David Buuck, 'African Doppelganger: Hybridity and Identity in the Work of Dambudzo Marechera,' *Research in African Literatures* 28, no. 2 (Summer 1997), 118.

by the very outspoken political meaning of his work, peppered with direct, allusive or symbolic references to colonialism, neo-colonialism, Rhodesia and Zimbabwe, despite its apparently chaotic refusal of plot and narrative direction.

But Marechera is unique in other ways, his short-lived career having an inordinate impact on the direction of African literature. It can be argued that Marechera broke the iron grip of realism in the African novel and paved the way for writers such as Ben Okri and others whose imaginative prose has more often been categorized as 'magical real.' Dambudzo Marechera's writing is not magical realism, but it so comprehensively fractures the tradition of realism that African writing could never be the same. Realism was important for the African novel for the simple reason that its original task of representing an African society to a global audience was to convince them that in fact African life was just as real as that of its readers. There is no better example of this than Chinua Achebe's *Things Fall Apart* (1958), the signal achievement of which was to combat the Conradian observation, in *Heart of Darkness* (1899), of Africans as a dehumanized otherness, 'a whirl of black limbs, a mass of hands clapping, of feet stamping, of bodies swaying, of eyes rolling, under the droop of heavy and motionless foliage.'[4] The primary achievement of Achebe's novel is its success in presenting the African village Umuofia as a real place and Okonkwo as a real human being. The representation of African society owes much to the realism of Achebe and Wole Soyinka, and also to Ngugi wa Thiong'o, whose later writing in works such as *Wizard of the Crow* (2006) breaks the realist tradition with a vengeance. Therefore, we can say that despite his short life and chaotic career, his wildly non-linear, non-narrative prose, Marechera paved the way for a different kind of African writing. He had certainly been foreshadowed to some extent by the linguistic adventurousness of Gabriel Okara and Ayi Kwei Armah, but Marechera's writing is so profoundly structurally

[4]   Joseph Conrad, *Heart of Darkness* (1899; London: Penguin, 2000), 62.

innovative, so resistant to the demands of story, that African writing could not ignore it.

One fascinating demonstration of Marechera's relationship with realism, one that acts out his continually reinvented biography and gives some insight perhaps into the porous border between fiction and reality, was an interview he gave Dutch journalist Alle Lansu in 1986. He says he was 11 years old and at home with his mother when his father was killed by a Rhodesian army officer. 'It was really horrible at the mortuary; you could see that he had been riddled with bullets, the heavy automatic bullets which had almost cut off a part of his body, because they had sewn it back, you could see the stitches.'[5] In fact, his father was run over by a car and Marechera, who was 11 at the time, was at boarding school. As Stewart Crehan asks, 'Is he giving a version he thinks will impress the interviewer? Has he genuinely confused fact and fiction? Or is he recreating a little boy's trauma?'[6] A number of answers to this are probably all plausible. Crehan answers himself that 'a key principle of Marecherian aesthetics is to blur fact and fiction and to fuse emotion and reality through techniques of distortion and dislocation.'[7] The 'fantastic dislocation' of his continually manufactured biography reveals an imbrication of Marechera's life and work that gives us an understanding of his writing in the Bakhtinian term 'Menippean,' an appellation that he preferred to the term 'African writer.'

The description 'Menippean' comes from Marechera's own pen. Many of the most interesting avenues into his writing come through his very sparse critical commentary, and one of the more interesting moves was his rejection of the title of 'African writer.' In an interview with Veit-Wild, he famously says:

5   Alle Lansu, 'Escape from the "House of Hunger:" Marechera Talks about His Life,' in *Dambudzo Marechera: A Source Book on his Life and Work*, 11.
6   Stewart Crehan, 'Review of Flora Veit-Wild *Dambudzo Marechera: A Source Book on his Life and Work*,' *Research in African Literatures* 25, no. 2 (Summer 1994), 198.
7   Ibid., 198.

I think I am the doppelganger whom, until I appeared, African literature had not yet met. And in this sense I would question anyone calling me an African writer. Either you are a writer or you are not. If you are a writer for a specific nation or a specific race, then fuck you. In other words, the direct international experience of every single entity is, for me, the inspiration to write.[8]

We are familiar with writers rejecting various categorizations of their writing. But Marechera's rejection of the term 'African writer' lies in the same category as other writers' rejection of nationality and offers an insight into a literature in the process of identifying itself as neither Eurocentric nor simply anti-colonial. Yet ironically, according to Pattison 'it is Marechera's refusal to accept an African literature and his desire to act on the world stage that, ironically, helps define his place in African literature.'[9] In a fascinating article, 'The African Writer's Experience of European Literature,' Marechera demonstrates not only his wide and sophisticated reading of European authors but also of his determination to belong to that company. 'From early in my life,' he says, 'I have viewed literature as a unique universe that has no internal divisions. I do not pigeon-hole it by race or language or nation. It is an ideal cosmos co-existing with this crude one.'[10]

We are likely to be highly suspicious of such sentiments these days, so tightly has Universalism been bound up with Eurocentric canonical ideas of literary value, and indeed, so dominant has it been in the concept of Literature itself. However disingenuous his protestations may be, clearly Marechera's 'universalism' fits more comfortably in the carnivalesque, Rabelaisian view of the chaotic excess of human life, the seething multifarious activity that lies below the level of Culture, and perhaps even

---

[8] Veit-Wild, *Dambudzo Marechera*, 121.

[9] David Pattison, 'Call No Man Happy: Inside *The Black Insider*, Marechera's Journey to Become a Writer?' *Journal of Southern African Studies* 20, no. 2 (June 1994), 222.

[10] Dambudzo Marechera, 'The African Writer's Experience of European Literature,' *Zambezia* 14, no. 2 (1987), 99.

below the 'Literary.' In this respect Marechera is a Menippean writer. It is very hard to approach his writing without using the term 'hybridity,'[11] not only in the sources of his influence but in the constant Biblical and cultural allusions that characterize his work. In refusing to be pigeonholed he alludes to a wide range of literature with which his own writing can be seen to be intertextual. Nevertheless, despite his protestations, Marechera's writing is African not only in setting but also in its combination of political protest and utopian projection.

For this and other reasons Marechera challenges our ways of categorizing writers. In rejecting even the title 'African writer' as a limiting and culturally isolating category, he reveals the demand for a different way of reading the African novel that was to come after his death in 1987 with the rise of post-colonial theory.[12] With the emergence of this new way of reading, the danger of a Manichean binary that quarantined 'African' writing on the cultural margins was to be obliterated by the concept of a rich tradition of literatures in English from formerly colonized societies. This was a way of reading those literatures that emphasized their transformative power as well as their difference. Despite Marechera's protestations that he was 'simply a writer,' there are writers and writers, every writer writes in a specific context, and post-colonial theory developed a reading practice to engage writers in their various milieus. The concerns of Marechera's work are readily accessible to post-colonial analysis but he had another solution to the problem of his potential Othering from European literature – Bakhtin's concept of carnival and Menippean satire. In an article published just before his death he says:

> Soviet critic Mikhail Bakhtin has offered a category of narrative whose unifying factor is a 'carnival' attitude to the world. This

---

[11] See Buuck, 'African Doppelganger.'

[12] See Bill Ashcroft, Gareth Griffiths and Helen Tiffin, *The Empire Writes Back: Theory and Practice in Post-colonial Literatures* (London: Routledge, 1989).

category includes writers from different backgrounds. They range from Aristophanes, Lucian and Apuleius (the first African novelist, perhaps) to Dostoevsky by way of Rabelais and Dean Swift. I add John Fowles and Günter Grass, and the Nigerian, Wole Soyinka, in *The Interpreters*. *Don Quixote* is quite at home. The world of such novels ... is complex, unstable, comic, satirical, fantastic, poetical and committed to the pursuit of truth. The hero can travel anywhere in this world and beyond. Fantasy and symbolism are combined with low-life naturalism. Odd vantage points offer changes of scale. Heaven and hell are close and may be visited. Madness, dreams and day-dreams, abnormal states of mind and all kinds of erratic inclinations are explored. Scandalous and eccentric behaviour disrupts 'the seemly course of human affairs' and provides a new view of 'the integrity of the world.' Society is unpredictable; roles can quickly change. Current affairs are treated with a satirical, journalistic interest. Genres are mixed. Stories, speeches, dramatic sketches, poetry and parody exist side by side. This category of novel is called the menippean. It is no longer necessary to speak of the African novel or the European novel: there is only the menippean novel.[13]

This is worth quoting at length because it offers a perfect description of the way Marechera saw his own writing. It would not be too ungenerous to say that Bakhtin gives Marechera's bizarre, chaotic, violent, allusive, ribald, prurient and scatological writing a place in the literary firmament. It presents 'odd vantage points [that] offer changes of scale;' we can definitely see the closeness of heaven and hell and the ability of the writer to visit them. 'Madness, dreams and day-dreams, abnormal states of mind and all kinds of erratic inclinations' are explored. Scandalous and eccentric behaviour disrupts 'the seemly course of human affairs' and provides a new view of 'the integrity of the world.'

So, the view of Marechera I am proposing is somewhat at variance with Veit-Wild's contention that 'the new postcolonial

---

[13] Marechera, 'The African Writer's Experience,' 101.

paradigm finally granted the formerly colonized the right to deviate from the image European anti-imperialists had formed of their "revolutionary subjects".'[14] That paradigm was yet to arrive when Marechera wrote, and to a great extent he preceded the rise of post-colonial analysis. While a strong relationship developed between Bakhtin and post-colonial theory, it tended to focus on dialogism and hybridity rather than the concepts of carnival and Menippean satire that Marechera claims for his writing. Bakhtin energizes Marechera's refusal of 'African' literature. 'It is no longer necessary,' he says, 'to speak of the African novel or the European novel: there is only the Menippean novel.'[15] And, indeed, the Menippean novel form seems a perfect fit for the idiosyncratic nature of his writing.

Despite the unruliness and rhizomic character of his narrative, Marechera's writing comprehensively fits Bakhtin's view of the novel, which for him, was not just another literary genre, but a special kind of force, which he calls 'novelness.' We know that Marechera was as much a poet as a fiction writer, thanks to Veit-Wild's collection *Cemetery of Mind*, and much of his fiction is in the form of short stories. But 'novelness' is relevant to his writing because he is what we might call a 'genre outlaw' *extraordinaire,* his novellas refusing to correspond to any traditional idea of the novel. Although *The House of Hunger* is categorized as short stories, it is as much an outlaw novel as *Black Sunlight.* And for Bakhtin the term 'novel' itself refers to 'whatever form of expression within a literary system reveals the limits of the system as inadequate, imposed or arbitrary.'[16] Paradoxically, given the importance of the novel within the literary canon, Bakhtin sees the novel as a kind of outlaw undermining the official or high culture of any society. The

---

[14] Flora Veit-Wild, 'Carnival and Hybridity in Texts by Dambudzo Marechera and Lesego Rampolokeng,' *Journal of Southern African Studies* 23, no. 4 (December 1997), 554.

[15] Marechera, 'The African Writer's Experience,' 101.

[16] Katerina Clark and Michael Holquist, *Mikhail Bakhtin* (Cambridge, Mass.: Harvard UP, 1984), 276.

features of official or high culture, inscribed in its literary, legal and religious texts, are undermined by the novel and its antecedents, and this is demonstrated in the Rabelaisian carnivalesque.

Opposed to the language of priests and monks, kings and seigneurs, knights and wealthy urban types, scholars and priests – to the languages of all who hold power and are set up well in life – there is the language of the merry rogue, wherever necessary parodically reproducing any pathos, always in such a way as to rob it of any power to harm... and thus turn what was a lie into a joyful deception.[17]

This identification of the novel as outlaw seems exaggerated today when we find so many novels perhaps confirming, rather than 'speaking truth to' power. But it remains true in the sense that 'novelness' cannot be confined within any clearly defined generic boundaries and the possibilities of the genre remain disparate and open-ended. The idea of the novel as outlaw is particularly relevant to Marechera whose writing often disrupts even the most basic requirements of narrative. But it is even more important in a literature that exists in the interstices of cultures, situated in the febrile and protean space offered by the post-colonial novel in an appropriated language. Marechera, leaving behind the measured political realism of earlier writers, becomes a Bakhtinian outlaw for both African and European cultures, taking the idea of the 'outlaw genre' to its post-colonial limits. It is all the more fascinating therefore, that he situated himself in the universal space of the 'writer.' But it becomes increasingly clear that the writer 'Dambudzo Marechera' stands firmly in the space opened up by Bakhtin's theory of the novel, of carnival, dialogism, heteroglossia, and the Menippean.

Bakhtin's unquestioned hero was Dostoyevsky, whose writing prompted him to develop the concept of polyphony with its related concepts of dialogism and heteroglossia.

---

[17] Mikhail Bakhtin, *The Dialogic Imagination*, ed. Michael Holquist, trans. Caryl Emerson and Michael Holquist (Austin: University of Texas Press, 1981), 301-2.

On the face of it, Marechera's writing often seems far from polyphonic, being an almost obsessive focus on the voice of the narrator and the construction of an inner world. But his writing becomes a fascinating demonstration of heteroglossia, evidencing Bakhtin's claim that the novel form itself provides a particularly rich medium for the many-voiced appearance of different languages:

> For the novelist working in prose, the object is always entangled in someone else's discourse about it, it is already present with qualifications, an object of dispute that is conceptualized and evaluated variously, inseparable from the heteroglot social apperception of it. The novelist speaks of this 'already qualified world' in a language that is heteroglot and internally dialogized. Thus both object and language are revealed to the novelist in their historical dimension, in the process of social and heteroglot becoming.[18]

Bakhtin is talking about a putatively monoglossic text, unhampered by the issues of cultural communication and cultural tension we find in the post-colonial novel. For him, such a text is already heteroglossic, already engaged in dialogue *within* the text, a dialogue, which to all intents and purposes, is a *cross-cultural* dialogue between 'belief systems.' In addition, the novel unifies its language and its world. 'For the novelist,' Bakhtin continues, 'there is no world outside his socioheteroglot perception – and there is no language outside the heteroglot intentions that stratify that world.'[19] Thus we might say that the novel is already a function of the meeting of many languages, all of which come with their own belief systems, a meeting that bodies forth fully the world of the novel.

We can find this heteroglossia even in Marechera's objection that the English in which he writes fractures his authentic world. Indeed the repetitive critique of English seems to be marked by a wry disingenuousness. 'The English language has

[18] Ibid., 330.
[19] Ibid., 330.

certainly taken over more than the geography of the African image,'[20] he complains, while liberally showering his writing with allusions and intertextual gestures to English and other European culture. 'I was a keen accomplice in my own mental colonization'[21] he says in his self interview. When he speaks about his bilingualism, which is more like the dialogism Bakhtin would call heteroglossia, he speaks of it in terms of brokenness and dislocation:

> I was being severed from my own voice. I would listen to it as a still, small voice coming from the huge distances of the mind. It was like this: English is my second language, Shona my first. When I talked it was in the form of an interminable argument, one side of which was always expressed in English and the other side always in Shona. At the same time I would be aware of myself as something indistinct but separate from both cultures.[22]

It is arguable that this 'brokenness' lies at the source of Marechera's choice to exile himself from both cultures, and in turn, to play out, both in his novels and the performance of his own life, the pathology of colonialism. Brokenness and 'deconstructedness' do indeed seem to operate at the level of subjectivity in Marechera, but mainly because the narrative structure is so relentlessly fragmented. The apparent performance of broken subjectivity in his writing is the consequence of a very intricately woven (though often confusing) Menippean structure. But even though the effect of his form and content is fragmenting, the subject of the novel can still be regarded in terms of variable subject positions, of 'layering' rather than disjunction. Despite their apparently disruptive 'anti-novelness,' his novellas are a stunning example of the heteroglossia Bakhtin regards as characteristic of the modern novel. The appropriation of English in the post-

[20] Marechera, *The Black Insider*, 49.
[21] Veit-Wild, *Dambudzo Marechera*, 4.
[22] Dambudzo Marechera, *The House of Hunger* (London: Heinemann, 1978), 30.

colonial text often leads to a transformation of the received language by the mother tongue. But it also becomes the meeting point of different traditions, different voices, and in this respect becomes an organic extension of Bakhtin's idea of novelness. This process becomes intensified in Marechera: in the passage above the resonant Biblical phrase 'still small voice' (one of the many Biblical, literary, and cultural allusions in his writing) enters seamlessly into the text, indicating a very different form of interaction between language cultures. The 'still small voice' is one amongst many as Marechera not only uses English but also employs a profusion of voices. The speech of Marechera's narrator is always *another's speech*. As Bakhtin says, 'Incorporated into the novel are a multiplicity of "language" and verbal-ideological belief systems … kept primarily within the limits of the literary written and conversational language.'[23]

The speech of Dostoyevsky's narrators, for instance, who are themselves characters, 'is always *another's speech* (as regards the real or potential direct discourse of the author) and in *another's language*.'[24] Bakhtin's term 'heteroglossia' counters the myth of authentic, 'faithful' language. All literary language is already multi-voiced, the author's 'intentions' already refracted through the multiple belief systems of the dialogic text. But consequently, the dialogue between author and narrator opens the way to consider all language as a multi-voiced space of translation. All forms involving a narrator:

> signify to one degree or another by their presence the author's free-dom from a unitary and singular language, a freedom connected with the relativity of literary and language systems; such forms open up the possibility of never having to define oneself in language, the possibility of translating one's own intentions from one linguistic system to another, of fusing 'the language of truth'

---

[23] Bakhtin, *The Dialogic Imagination*, 311.
[24] Ibid., 324.

with 'the language of everyday,' of saying 'I am me' in someone else's language, and in my own language 'I am other.'[25]

The dual dynamic of saying 'I am me' in another's language and 'I am other' in my own language captures precisely the dual achievement of the second language writer. For such a writer, while emphasizing the way in which the space between author and reader is closed within the demands of meanability, also demonstrates in heightened form, the writer's negotiation of the forces brought to bear on language. Add to this the prolific intertextuality of Marechera's writing and we find an extravagant heteroglossia both enacted and represented.

The cognate term here is *intertextuality* and we see this in profusion throughout the writing. Take the following long passage in which the narrator of *Black Sunlight* is running away after having been hung upside down in a chicken coop:

It flashed right through me, the history of the Runner. Another spear nicked my hip. Fucking Allah! And there was Hitler at the Olympic Games turning his backside on our finest athlete. You do not wait for the starter's gun. The mere presence of the Ku-Klux-Klan in the neighbourhood is enough. Or the National Front. The mere presence of the fucking pigs is enough to catapult one to the other side of the earth. Motherfucking Buddha! I've spent my life running from one bit of earth to another. Carrying my smashed peace of mind into the oddest gangs of peoples. Take this one for instance. I bring them music and laughter and poetry and they throw me into a pitlatrine. By now Blanche can already smell my inglorious flight, covered in humanshit, chickenshit and prickling all over with ghastly spears. Stanley meets Mutesa. Blanche Goodfather I presume. I am a bit of alright, Blanche, just a slight case of black wasps I trod on. You know. A nip into the pool will quickly restore me to my old self. Fucking military arse! Another spear just shaved off my right sideboard. The persistent bastards. I'm only a fucking court jester, Chief, not a dissident like

---

[25] Ibid., 314-15.

Sakharov. Shit. The spears are still flying. I wonder if Walter Mitty ever daydreamed anything like this? There are more immediate things in the world than all my travel and Oxford degree. As I fought through a stubborn tangle of ropelike undergrowth, getting scratched, gouged, gagged, entangled, I thought of Sparta and Athens and how the runner got through. I fought thicker and thicker into the mass of thorny vines. I heard running feet. They seemed to come from every side. It was black. I simply stood perfectly still right in the middle of that now - I hoped - blessed hideous undergrowth.[26]

In running away he becomes every dissident, outcast, outlaw, escapee in history – a flight described with an ebullient Rabelaisian humour. The passage amplifies the dialogism that is fundamental to the novel and which Marechera demonstrates in excessive profusion. 'For the prose writer,' Bakhtin writes,

the object is a focal point for heteroglot voices among which his own voice must also sound; these voices create the background necessary for his own voice, outside of which his artistic prose nuances cannot be perceived, and without which they 'do not sound.'[27]

The passage above is not simply heteroglossic, but the demonstration of a determined and excessive intertextuality that seems to exist primarily to pronounce its own intertextual exuberance. Intertextuality is a useful term introduced by Julia Kristeva in her study of Bakhtin and brilliantly elaborated by Todorov.[28] It becomes particularly relevant to Marechera in whose writing we find not just dialogism and heteroglossia but a radically *performative* intertextuality that is fundamental to the Menippean disruptiveness of his narrative. The chaotic exuberance of Marechera's generic structures have led many to

---

[26] Dambudzo Marechera, *Black Sunlight* (London: Heinemann, 1980), 9.

[27] Bakhtin, *The Dialogic Imagination*, 278.

[28] See Tzvetan Todorov, *Mikhail Bakhtin: The Dialogical Principle*, trans. Wlad Godzich (Minneapolis: University of Minneapolis Press, 1984).

see a focus in the 'I' of the text, to read it as an elaboration on Marechera's own constantly manufactured subjectivity. But his appeal to the genre of Menippean satire, if we look closely, is an extremely useful way to understand his work because it easily incorporates the interlocking weave of Marechera's various invented selves.

In his 'Problems of Dostoyevsky's Poetics,' Bakhtin discusses genre as a stable yet constantly transforming tendency in literature's development. Genre is 'reborn and renewed at every new stage'[29] and the archaic elements of their origin are always capable of renewing themselves. He identifies three fundamental roots to the novelistic genre: the epic, the rhetorical and the carnivalistic, and the roots of the line that leads to the dialogic character of the Dostoyevskian novel are the Socratic dialogue and Menippean satire. 'This carnivalized genre,' he says,

> extraordinarily flexible and as changeable as Proteus, capable of penetrating other genres, has had an enormous and as yet insufficiently appreciated importance for the development of European literatures. Menippean satire became one of the main carriers and channels for the carnival sense of the world in literature, and remains so to the present day.[30]

It may be stating the obvious to see Marechera's work as an exuberant demonstration of the carnivalesque, but it does provide us with a view of his writing as not so much subverting the novel form as realizing its dialogic potential. Marechera's claim upon the category 'Menippean' may or may not reflect a conscious impulse in the writing, but it does provide a valuable analytical framework. The section on Menippean satire occupies only a few pages of Bakhtin's discussion of Dostoyevsky's poetics but it offers a prodigious range of characteristics, most of which correspond to Marechera's work in an uncanny way.

[29] Pam Morris, ed., *The Bakhtin Reader: Selected Writings of Bakhtin, Medvedev, Voloshinov* (London: Edward Arnold, 1984), 188.
[30] Ibid., 189.

In summary, Bakhtin sees the Menippean as constituted by the following:

1) *Extraordinary freedom of plot and philosophical invention.*[31]

2) *The use of the fantastic to test an idea.* According to Bakhtin the 'bold and unrestrained use of the fantastic and adventure is internally motivated, justified by and devoted to a purely ideational and philosophical end: the creation of extraordinary situations for the provoking and testing of a philosophical idea, a discourse, a truth.'[32]

3) *Slum Naturalism.* The 'organic combination within it of the free fantastic, the symbolic, at times even a mystical-religious element with an extreme and (from our point of view) crude *slum naturalism.* The adventures of truth on earth take place on the high road, in brothels, in the dens of thieves, in taverns, marketplaces, prisons, in the erotic orgies of secret cults, and so forth. The idea here fears no slum, is not afraid of any of life's filth. The man of the idea – the wise man – collides with worldly evil, depravity, baseness, and vulgarity in their most extreme expression. This slum naturalism is apparently already present in the earliest menippea....'[33]

4) *Philosophical Universalism:* 'Boldness of invention and the fantastic element are combined in the menippea with an extraordinary philosophical universalism and a capacity to contemplate the world on the broadest possible scale. Menippea is a genre of "ultimate questions." In it ultimate philosophical positions are put to the test.'[34]

5)   *Moral – psychological experimentation:* 'a representation of the unusual, abnormal moral and psychic states of man - insanity of all sorts (the theme of the maniac), split personality, unrestrained

[31] Ibid., 188.
[32] Ibid., 189.
[33] Ibid., 190.
[34] Ibid., 190.

daydreaming, unusual dreams, passions bordering on madness, suicides, and so forth. These phenomena do not function narrowly in the menippea as mere themes, but have a formal generic significance. Dreams, daydreams, insanity destroy the epic and tragic wholeness of a person and his fate: the possibilities of another person and another life are revealed in him, he loses his finalized quality and ceases to mean only one thing; he ceases to coincide with himself.'[35]

6) *Scandal and eccentricity*: 'Scandal scenes, eccentric behavior, inappropriate speeches and performances, that is, all sorts of violations of the generally accepted and customary course of events and the established norms of behavior and etiquette, including manners of speech.'[36]

7) *Sharp contrasts and oxymoronic combinations.*[37]

8) *Inserted genres.* 'A wide use of inserted genres: novellas, letters, oratorical speeches, symposia … a mixing of prose and poetic speech. The inserted genres are presented at various distances from the ultimate authorial position.'[38]

9) *Concern with current and topical issues.*[39]

Anyone who is at all familiar with Marechera's work can see immediately the relevance of all these characteristics to his writing, the novelness of which is not diminished by being published as short stories. Plots are often so dislocated and the fragmentation of his prose so extreme as to completely disrupt any demand for narrative coherence. At times the writing has the appearance of the structure of dream, where changes in plot hinge on an image or a word, launching into a totally different time and place. More often the plot circles in ever

[35] Ibid., 191.
[36] Ibid., 191.
[37] Ibid., 191.
[38] Ibid., 192.
[39] Ibid., 192.

diminishing circles, at points where the character in one event becomes the occasion for another story or the description of an event. At one point an old man tells a story that has all the characteristics of traditional mythic narrative: about a man who brought his wife home an egg which she loved and during the night she gave birth to a giant egg.[40] This kind of dream-like fragmentation of narrative is one that offers a discourse of philosophical universalism because it allows a prodigious breadth of imagination to take in Marechera's unconventional view of the human condition.

The Black Insider, which seems to be the first recognizably novelistic narrative, is characterized by a Menippean variety of genres – fiction, poetry, dramatic dialogue. It stretches the category 'novel' in various other ways, despite its apparent linearity. Sometimes the prose consists of collections of aphorisms:

> That joke can cure a cobra's bite. Whatever we achieve is the evidence of our guilt. Always we are the desert island for which we secretly pine. There is nowhere to hide on the road to suicide.[41]

The autonomy of each of these sentences has the same effect on reading as poetry, slowing it down, demanding reflection, and it is significant that poetry, in *Cemetery of Mind* forms such a substantial part of Marechera's oeuvre. Indeed what seems like genre transgression in the prose seems natural in poetry. The 'extraordinary freedom of plot and philosophical invention' can often be seen therefore in changes from sentence to sentence as the narrative changes direction.

The presence of 'slum naturalism,' scandal and eccentricity, a penchant for sharp contrasts and oxymoronic combinations are everywhere present in Marechera's writing but they proliferate in the scatological and prurient, in what Kristeva terms the 'abject.' This refers to the human reaction (horror,

---

[40] Marechera, *The House of Hunger*, 80-81.
[41] Marechera, *The Black Insider*, 38.

vomit) to a threatened breakdown in meaning caused by the loss of the distinction between subject and object or between self and other. The primary reminder of our own materiality is the corpse; but the same reaction is generated by our human detritus: things such as an open wound, shit, sewage, dead skin, even the skin that forms on the surface of warm milk. Kristeva writes that the abject is 'radically excluded' and 'draws me toward the place where meaning collapses.'[42] Indeed, it is the abject and the scatological that define the often scathingly dystopian character of Marechera's world. It is precisely this surface corporeality that presents the writer's sense of a collapse of meaning.

The abject, which may be the most common demonstration of the corporeal nature of humanity is also the region that suggests the character of human pointlessness. Marechera, despite his interest in topical issues, is concerned with humanity in all its secretions and abjection:

> There is nothing to make one particularly glad one is a human being and not a horse, or a lion, or a jackal, or come to think of it a snake. Snakes. There's just dirt and shit and urine and blood and smashed brains. There's dust and fleas and bloody whites and roaches and dogs trained to bite black people in the arse. There's venereal disease and beer and lunacy and just causes. There's technology to drop on your head wherever you stop to take a leak. There's white shit in our leaders and white shit in our dreams and white shit in our history and white shit on our hands and in anything we build or pray for.[43]

The abject for Marechera is also that region in which our humanity itself becomes open to question. Kristeva refers to the primitive effort to separate ourselves from the animal. 'By way of abjection,' she writes, 'primitive societies have

---

[42] Julia Kristeva, *Powers of Horror: An Essay on Abjection*, trans. Leon S. Roudiez (New York: Columbia UP, 1982), 2.
[43] Marechera, *The House of Hunger*, 58.

marked out a precise area of their culture in order to remove it from the threatening world of animals or animalism, which were imagined as representatives of sex and murder.'[44] But interestingly, the above passage from 'House of Hunger' suggests the abject as the region in which our distinction from animals breaks down. The abject seems to proliferate in Marechera's writing, then, because it is the point at which meaning, humanity, and identity become radically destabilized. So rather than simply trying to shock, the writing employs the abject (whether consciously or not) as a common scene of Menippean transgression.

Marechera's writing is violent, scatalogical and pessimistic and we could track through the Bakhtinian definition to find precise correlations in Marechera's writing for each characteristic. But the feature of Menippean satire that seems to offer a key to the deepest impulses of his work is the use of the fantastic in order to test an idea. Despite the dystopian character of his writing, Marechera's *vision* is decidedly utopian, and the idea that his fantastic narratives test (and enact) is the very possibility of *freedom*. Early in 'House of Hunger' the narrator says

> The freedom we craved for – as one craves for dagga or beer or cigarettes or the after-life – this was so alive in our breath and in our fingers that one became intoxicated by it even before one had actually found it. It was like the way a man licks his lips in his dream of a feast; the way a woman dances in her dream of a carnival; the way the old man ran like a gazelle in his yearning for the funeral games of his youth. Yet the feast, the carnival and the games were not there at all. This was the paradox whose discovery left us uneasy, sly and at best with the ache of knowing that one would never feel that way again. There were no conscious farewells to adolescence for the emptiness was deep-seated in the gut. We knew that before us lay another vast emptiness whose appetite for things living was at best wolfish. Life stretched out like a series of hunger-scoured hovels stretching endlessly towards the

---

[44] Kristeva, *Powers of Horror*, 12-13.

horizon. One's mind became the grimy rooms, the dusty cobwebs in which the minute skeletons of one's childhood were forever in the spidery grip that stretched out to include not only the very stones upon which we walked but also the stars which glittered vaguely upon the stench of our lives.[45]

This is an existential freedom that goes beyond the desire for the overthrow of colonial rule, although we see the constant presence of violent oppression as a 'concern with current topical issues' that characterizes Menippean satire. It is a freedom lying deep within the soul – a utopianism that goes hand in hand, perhaps necessarily, with his break from the realism of the African novel. The Menippean form *enacts* – while representing – the freedom that lies on his horizon. Marechera holds fiercely to his gloomy view of life: 'Don't get me wrong. I'm a pessimist, but I still add two and two and walk to the seven, smiling.'[46] But despite the fact that he bangs his head against the wall of life until the 'whole Earth is one big headache'[47] inside his head nevertheless the vision of freedom remains the enduring core of the utopianism of his work.

Ernst Bloch defines the utopian in terms of the 'anticipatory consciousness' common to all human life. Yet Marechera's work is itself a form of anticipation – an anticipation of the utopian that was to flourish in African writing. Marechera wrote at a time after the 1960s when 'the failure of independence became the overriding theme of African literature.'[48] African writers were the first to recognize that the emancipatory potential of independence had been at the very least, overestimated, and more often simply betrayed. If we consider novels such as Achebe's *A Man of the People* (1966), Soyinka's *The Interpreters*

---

[45] Marechera, *The House of Hunger*, 3-4.
[46] Ibid., 58.
[47] Ibid., 59.
[48] Paul Tiyambe Zeleza, 'The Democratic Transition in Africa and the Anglophone Writer,' *Canadian Journal of African Studies/Revue Canadienne des Études Africaines* 28, no. 3 (1994), 482.

(1965), and Armah's trilogy of despair *The Beautyful Ones Are Not Yet Born* (1968), *Fragments* (1970), *Why Are We So Blest?* (1972) and many other novels of these decades including Ngugi's *Petals of Blood* (1977) and *Devil on the Cross* (1982), we might well wonder what place utopianism really had in this litany of protest. Yet these novels, which reject both the imperial presence and its colonial inheritance in distorted nationalisms, provide the very critique on which the imagination of a better future can be built.

Armah's trilogy, for instance gives way to a series of novels that celebrate the pharaonic heritage of African culture, a utopian move that revealed the importance of memory to the new African movement that coincided, fascinatingly, with the move away from realism in the novel. Another writer who demonstrates this is Ben Okri, whose writing career could be said to be a reflection of the progress of African literature from dismay at the chaos of post-independence states to dreams of the future. His early fiction explores the political violence he witnessed during the civil war in Nigeria. His first two novels, *Flowers and Shadows* (1980) and *The Landscapes Within* (1981), are both set in Nigeria and feature as central characters two young men struggling to make sense of the disintegration and chaos happening in both their family and country. But the trilogy begun with *The Famished Road* (1991) which was continued into *Songs of Enchantment* (1993) and *Infinite Riches* (1998) offers a very different vision of Africa, presented in what appears to be a 'magical real' style, a state in which the allegorical, the material and the spirit realm are in constant interaction. Yet another example of this move occurs in Ngugi's later novels, particularly *Wizard of the Crow*, in which an exuberant and excessive satire lambastes post-independence African rule with a utopian edge of fantastic parody.

Marechera fits into this development in an interesting way. Writing within what may be called the period of deepest disillusion in African literature, and absorbing that disillusion into his sense of the corporeal abjection of life, he nevertheless anticipated the utopianism of African literature that began to emerge late in the century through his use of the extravagant and carnivalesque enactment of freedom. This, then, is no simple utopianism. It involves a psychological *intopia* in which the promise of a flowering of freedom brings together the psychological and political:

> I looked up. As I did so the old cloth of my former self seemed to stretch and tear once more. The pain flashed through my head and like a cold hand squeezed my bloody lungs. (What shall I see when the cloth rips completely, laying everything bare? It is as if a crack should appear in the shell of the sky ... And what of the house inside it? And the thing inside the house? And the thing inside the thing inside the thing inside the thing? I was drunk, I suppose, orbiting around myself shamelessly. I found a seed, a little seed, the smallest in the world. And its name was Hate. I buried it in my mind and watered it with tears. No seed ever had a better gardener. As it swelled and cracked into green life I felt my nation tremble, tremble in the throes of birth-and burst out bloom and branch).[49]

Hate, tears — surely we are witnessing a damaged and dystopian internal world. But the image of the seed is an image of hope because the flowering of resistance is a flowering of freedom. A vision of utopian freedom is painful because it is a vision delayed, and thus the conception of utopia is always critical. But it is *freedom* that lies in the future, a freedom demonstrated in every line of Marechera's prose — an *anarchism* of style that embodies the freedom he seeks. It is in this anarchism, no doubt, that binds the writing and the life. This is the idea tested by the fantastic dimensions of Marechera's prose: the idea of freedom.

In line with his prediction of this utopian development in African literature, hope exists only in flashes and glimmers in

[49] Marechera, *The House of Hunger*, 17.

the writing, which, even when offering an allegorical dimension, as in *The Black Insider*, still shows the inner pathology, the psychological damage caused by a violent world. When a strange girl tries to kill him he reasons, 'I don't know how but I go it into my thick skull that it was not the war but the invisible wounds bleeding in her mind which made her like that.'[50] One of the most fascinating features of the emergence of a new utopianism in African writing is its coincidence with a move beyond the realism that had characterized the early novel. Ben Okri's *Infinite Riches,* for instance, is an attempt to show the scope of cultural possibility by infusing the language of excess with the enormously expanded vision of the horizons of African cultural experience. In this sense Okri's and other contemporary African writing is no longer 'writing back' but creating a new imaginative universe. Perhaps no other writer inhabits this universe as completely as Dambudzo Marechera.

Looking back now upon Marechera's work we can see that this universe has its seeds in the Menippean excess of his writing. An all-consuming heteroglossic novelness, an exuberant Rabelaisian carnivalism, and a range of features that correspond closely to Bakhtin's definition of Menippean satire, are all evidence of a restless, rebellious and innovative imagination. The cost of this was exile – 'I have been an outsider in my own biography, in my country's history, in the world's terrifying possibilities.'[51] Perhaps it was a necessary exile that Marechera played out in the dual fictions of his life and work. His writing thus uniquely combines the pathology of colonialism with the exuberant possibilities of a post-colonial imagination. However necessary, however self-imposed his exile, the recognition of his place at the turning point of African literature may bring him 'home' to his rightful place in post-colonial studies.

---

[50] Marechera, *The Black Insider*, 28.
[51] Marechera, 'The African Writer's Experience,' 102.

6

Black but not Fanon
Reading *The Black Insider*

DAVID HUDDART

My skin sticks out a mile in all the crowds around here. Every time I go out I feel it tensing up, hardening, torturing itself. It only relaxes when I am in shadow, when I am alone, when I wake up early in the morning, when I am doing mechanical actions, and, strangely enough, when I am angry. But it is coy and self-conscious when I draw in my chair and begin to write. – Dambudzo Marechera, 'Black Skin What Mask.'[1]

O my body, make of me always a man who questions! – Frantz Fanon, *Black Skin, White Masks*.[2]

Having encountered Dambudzo Marechera's work, readers may express broadly similar responses, even if those responses are immediately qualified or rejected. For example, the generic status of his works, so often apparently autobiographical, becomes a source of concern that leads various commentators to insist that his works are definitely not self-obsessed: David Pattison writes that, 'I stress the personal and idiosyncratic nature of Marechera's writing but argue that such an approach was neither exclusive nor narcissistic.'[3] Then, of course, it is fairly suggested that his work is not only individualistic but is in fact unique. So, to take but one example, according to Brian Evenson,[4] Marechera on his own constitutes 'Zimbabwe's

[1] Dambudzo Marechera, 'Black Skin What Mask,' in *The House of Hunger* (London: Heinemann, 1978), 93.
[2] Frantz Fanon, *Black Skin, White Masks*, trans. Charles Lam Markmann (1967; London: Pluto Press, 1986), 232.
[3] David Pattison, 'Call No Man Happy: Inside *The Black Insider*, Marechera's Journey to Become a Writer?' *Journal of Southern African Studies* 20, no. 2 (June 1994), 222.
[4] Brian Evenson, 'Zimbabwe's Beat Generation,' in *Thus Spake the Corpse: An Exquisite*

Beat Generation.' Yet this example immediately throws up an obvious qualification to Marechera's uniqueness: he is constantly comparing himself, and inviting his readers to compare him, with other literary figures. Dambudzo Marechera is most certainly 'allusive Marechera,' suggesting that however self-obsessed he may be, his self-obsession is constantly channeled through the work of other writers; however striking his work can be at the sentence level, there are numerous influences and affiliations that help us understand how to read his writing. Indeed, reading Marechera's *The Black Insider* prompts us to consider his relation to any number of writers: Wilde, Achebe, Shelley, Burroughs, and so on. Indeed, so many are the allusions that in her introduction, Flora Veit-Wild feels compelled to insist that the novel's allusiveness is more than showy gimmickry. Various other chapters in this volume demonstrate the very real connections between Marechera's work and other important writers, and as readers we need to take his allusions seriously.

Of course, there are also 'non-literary' writers to whom Marechera refers, but these examples are either apparently too brief or too predictable, and are easy to ignore or interpret straightforwardly. One such example is Roland Barthes, mentioned in *The Black Insider*, and also on the first page of Marechera's widely-read essay, 'An African Writer's Experience of European Literature.' Reflecting on Barthes' criticism of objectivity, Marechera ruefully comments that, 'he will probably find himself falling into oblivion without a parachute.'[5] Barthes' fragmented and autobiographical critical forms have clear appeal to Marechera, but he also recognizes the danger of dismissal inherent in such a fragmented critical perspective. A second central example, Frantz Fanon, could be read alongside

---

(contd) *Corpse Reader 1988-1998 vol. 2*, Andrei Codrescu and Laura Rosenthal (eds) (Santa Rosa, CA: Black Sparrow Press, 1999), 357-9.

5 Dambudzo Marechera, *The Black Insider*, ed. Flora Veit-Wild (London: Lawrence and Wishart, 1990), 123. Unless indicated otherwise, further page references are in the main text.

Barthes, but instead has been read through Marechera to understand the double-voicedness, the paranoia, and the psychical split consequent upon colonialism, as explored in Marechera's evidently fragmented fiction. Further than that, like many literary writers, Fanon is clear-eyed about the dangers of the postcolonial period. As Annie Gagiano suggests, Fanon understands, as creative writers do, 'how complex and deep a healing process is required in the aftermath of colonialism, and how easily this can go wrong.'[6] Such readings of Fanon are predictable in a positive sense: they are necessary and helpful extrapolations from remarks Marechera himself makes. In his discussion of European influence on African literature, Marechera simply asks: 'How can Africa write as if that Black Frenchman, Franz [sic] Fanon, never existed – I refer to the Fanon of *Black Skin, White Mask* [sic].'[7] Fanon constitutes a kind of limit example for those critics who would purge European influence, and Marechera knows how absurd it would be to exclude Fanon from an 'African canon.' In *The Black Insider*, for another example, one of the fragmented narrators suffers an ever-present violence, and he is sent off to seek psychoanalytic help: 'Finally, a psychology lecturer suggested that I see an analyst. I did. But I never quite knew how he'd cured me. He was black, but he wasn't Frantz Fanon' (130-1). Again, archness notwithstanding, Marechera is presenting us with a Fanon we know and understand, even if it is a sometimes controversial version of the great revolutionary psychiatrist: responses to Homi Bhabha's reading,[8] which of course puts such stress on *Black Skin, White Masks* at the expense of *The Wretched of the Earth*, demonstrate the potential controversy of putting too much stress on the psychical at the expense of the political. However, it is arguable that the connection between Marechera

6 Annie Gagiano, *Achebe, Head, Marechera: On Power and Change in Africa* (Boulder, CO: Lynne Rienner, 2000), 32.

7 Dambudzo Marechera, 'The African Writer's Experience of European Literature,' *Zambezia* 14, no. 2 (1987), 100.

8 See Homi K. Bhabha, *The Location of Culture* (London: Routledge, 1994).

and Fanon can be reimagined as a comparison. I suggest, then, that Fanon is just as playful with genre as Marechera, and to similar ends in terms of identity: Fanon's theory can be understood as a kind of life-writing, as Bart Moore-Gilbert has recently argued,[9] and Marechera's autobiographical fictions can themselves be understood as a kind of theory.

If we are to understand what is happening in Marechera's work, it is clearly necessary to think about the genre of auto-biography. Marechera himself told many stories about his life, in life, and in work, and at all times maintained a healthy disdain for any reader willing to see every work as autobiographical:

> There are those who find in memory the evidence of their identity; indeed, some say each individual is himself the microcosm of all that mankind has been from the beginning of time. But perhaps this is to be seduced by metaphors - an act of self-mystification which beguiles those writers and readers for whom every novel or poem is seen as autobiography.[10]

Already, here, Marechera is putting into question any writer, or anyone at all, willing to put themselves forward as exemplary. And yet of course, it is difficult for us to entirely dismiss our ideas about exemplarity, or even just being an example, when we come to a writer like Marechera, who lived a life such as his. Indeed, there are different versions of exemplarity, just as there are different versions of the autobiographical, as Sidonie Smith and Julia Watson remind us, 'The autobiographical exceeds attempts to pigeonhole it, in terms of generic aesthetics, forms, usages, and receptions.'[11] This excess is constitutive of exemplarity as such, and Marechera himself is not entirely

---

[9] See Bart Moore-Gilbert, *Postcolonial Life-Writing: Culture, Politics and Self-Representation* (London: Routledge, 2009).

[10] Dambudzo Marechera, 'Soyinka, Dostoevsky: the Writer on Trial for his Time,' *Zambezia* 14, no. 2 (1987), 106-7.

[11] Sidonie Smith and Julia Watson, 'The Trouble with Autobiography: Cautionary Notes for Narrative Theorists,' in *A Companion to Narrative Theory*, James Phelan and Peter Rabinowitz (eds) (Oxford: Blackwell, 2005), 357.

dismissive of exemplarity; indeed, ambivalence on this point makes life-writing of a sort the most appropriate genre for him. This appropriateness can be more clearly understood through considering Jacques Derrida's classic essay 'The Law of Genre.'

Discussing what he calls '*the law of* the law of genre,' Derrida specifically reminds us that this law is about exemplarity: 'What is at stake, in effect, is exemplarity and its whole *enigma.*'[12] Indeed, much of what Derrida has to say about genre applies equally well to questions about autobiography, as has been argued on a number of occasions,[13] and as we will explore again a little later. Derrida's formulation of the law of the law is as follows:

> a principle of contamination, a law of impurity, a parasitical economy. In the code of set theories, if I may use it at least figuratively, I would speak of a sort of participation without belonging - a taking part in without being part of, without having membership in a set.[14]

This discussion has an intuitive attraction to postcolonial theory, in its formulation of a kind of hybridity, but its use is more specific, and precisely derives from this treatment of exemplarity as enigmatic. In a lengthy and complex discussion, Irene E. Harvey criticizes Derrida for a rigid either/or conception of exemplarity, in which exemplarity simply goes unthought: 'the rhetoric of "exemplary" or "exemplary" used rhetorically, does nothing other than conceptualize, make lawful, based on nothing but the performativity of itself. I made it, and I said that it was good. And it was good.'[15] However, as will also be seen with Marechera, in terms of the discussion of genre, it is

---

[12] Jacques Derrida, 'The Law of Genre,' *Critical Inquiry* 7, no. 1 (Autumn 1980), 59.

[13] See, for example, Robert Smith, *Derrida and Autobiography* (Cambridge: Cambridge UP, 1995); David Huddart, *Postcolonial Theory and Autobiography* (London: Routledge, 2008); and, Moore-Gilbert, *Postcolonial Life-Writing.*

[14] Derrida, 'The Law of Genre,' 59.

[15] Irene E. Harvey, *Labyrinths of Exemplarity: At the Limits of Deconstruction* (Albany: State University of New York Press, 2002), 199.

clearly insufficient to see Derrida's thought as structured by an opposition between being a minority of one and being a fully signed-up member of the clan.

This point becomes clear if we compare this law of genre with a kind of law of cultural identity that Derrida outlines in relation to Europe, as found in *The Other Heading*:

> I am European, I am no doubt a European intellectual, and I like to recall this, I like to recall this to myself, and why would I deny it? In the name of what? But I am not, nor do I feel, European *in every part*, that is, European through and through. By which I mean, by which I wish to say, or *must* say: I do not want to be and must not be European through and through, European *in every part*. Being a part, belonging as 'fully a part,' should be incompatible with belonging 'in every part.'[16]

It is possible to construe this passage as Derrida recalling his Algerian identity, and this construal could be cross-referenced with his discussion of identity in, for example, *Monolingualism of the Other*. According to this reading, when he presents himself as exemplary, it is just as Harvey suggests: 'I am exemplary, because I say I am.' However, in that later text, Derrida does in fact think through the performative implications at some length, and as can be seen in the passages on genre and Europe, the logic he outlines is not just an acknowledgement that some people have hybrid 'heritage.' According to this logic, a logic of exemplarity which is of participation without belonging, there is a solidified and very 'serious' aspect to so-called pure belonging which is inappropriate to a politics worthy of the name. Derrida indeed enjoins us to take the name 'Europe' simultaneously seriously and lightly, and it is possible to imagine such a suggestion being applied to 'Africa' too. Again, Marechera would recognize this possibility, and we certainly find 'Africa' given this double treatment in his work. And as in

---

[16] Jacques Derrida, *The Other Heading: Reflections on Today's Europe*, trans. Pascale-Anne Brault and Michael B. Naas (Bloomington: Indiana UP, 1992), 82.

the case of Derrida, there is a logical connection between this cultural identity and the question of genre, which again is why autobiographical forms are so appropriate to his project.

In now focusing on autobiography, or more broadly life-writing, I am following a path that other critics have taken in reading Marechera. Melissa Levin and Laurice Taitz, for example, suggest that his autobiographical forms are an appropriate vehicle for his understanding of identity. They write, 'The implications of Marechera's work are that identity is not a fixed or stable category, but is in essence unstable, fluid, and ever-changing and necessitates constant redefinition.'[17] In this reading of his playful use of autobiography, Levin and Taitz are confirming more general readings of Marechera's narrative technique, concisely expressed by Drew Shaw:

> In the text it is as if Marechera speaks with two voices, his narrative of what he sees is ruptured by his thoughts which penetrate beneath the surface layer of representation. His double-voicedness is also deliberate in that it represents his refusal to create an authoritarian, monologic, seamless text.[18]

As I mentioned earlier, this analysis of narrative double-voicedness is almost self-evident, but no less important for that. Additionally, it allows critics to cross-reference Marechera's work with that of Fanon, who provides such fertile theorization of psychical splitting under colonialism and its aftermath. Nonetheless, there is more to be said about the connection with Fanon, as I have already suggested, and as other critics have begun to argue.

One example is Moore-Gilbert, who suggests, as other commentators have noted, that *Black Skin, White Masks* is a

[17] Melissa Levin and Laurice Taitz, 'Fictional Autobiographies or Autobiographical Fictions?' in *Emerging Perspectives on Dambudzo Marechera*, Flora Veit-Wild and Anthony Chennells (eds) (Trenton, NJ: Africa World Press, 1999), 163.

[18] Drew Shaw, 'Transgressing Traditional Narrative Form,' in *Emerging Perspectives on Dambudzo Marechera*, 37.

fundamentally hybrid text. Moore-Gilbert goes further than this, suggesting that, 'its discourse ranges between the modes of scientific analysis, confession and poetry, and between the oral and the literary – all within a structure which is sometimes highly fragmented and imagistic.'[19] In this, Fanon anticipates the formal innovations of more recent autobiographical writers of many persuasions, but specifically postcolonial life-writers. The aspect of Fanon's work that Moore-Gilbert highlights which is of most interest here, though, is its future-orientation. Of course, this orientation is clearly present in Fanon's analysis of Négritude, for example: 'Those Negroes and white men will be disalienated who refuse to let themselves be sealed away in the materialized Tower of the Past.'[20] As Robert Bernasconi suggests, 'Fanon is unwilling to look to the past of peoples of colour for a solution or for his "original calling".'[21] This analysis appears to require a rejection of the past, but not necessarily the outright embrace of the future, as might be understood in the following passage:

> Every human problem must be considered from the standpoint of time. Ideally, the present will always contribute to the building of the future. And this future is not the future of the cosmos but rather the future of my century, my country, my existence. In no fashion should I undertake to prepare the world that will come later. I belong irreducibly to my time. And it is for my own time that I should live.[22]

As one would expect in the work of such a situated and revolutionary thinker, particularly one who would later write and act in such a concrete manner, the standpoint of time is not allowed to become abstract. However, as Fanon immediately

---

[19] Moore-Gilbert, *Postcolonial Life-Writing*, 71.

[20] Fanon, *Black Skin, White Masks*, 226.

[21] Robert Bernasconi, 'The Assumption of Negritude: Aimé Césaire, Frantz Fanon, and the Vicious Circle of Racial Politics,' *Parallax* 8, no. 2 (2002), 73.

[22] Fanon, *Black Skin, White Masks*, 13.

goes on to write, 'The future should be an edifice supported by living men. This structure is connected to the present to the extent that I consider the present in terms of something to be exceeded.'[23] Exceeding the present is of course where this text concludes: 'I should constantly remind myself that the real *leap* consists in introducing invention into existence.'[24] The connection made by Moore-Gilbert between this orientation and the form of Fanon's text is particularly suggestive since the text is involved in a constant 'leaping,' rather like *The Black Insider*.

When comparing Fanon with Marechera, it is important to remember just how much formal diversity there is in Fanon's work. I would certainly not make too direct a formal comparison between Marechera and *The Wretched of the Earth*. However, postcolonial theory has returned to an earlier Fanon, and this Fanon is more clearly connected with Marechera's fragmentation. One of the numerous striking characteristics of *Black Skin, White Masks* is its refusal to remain within one discourse, to stick to one approach to its defined problem. It switches rapidly between autobiographical reflection, psychoanalytic literary criticism, and phenomenology. Additionally, there are the numerous footnotes that often cast the body of the text in a different light. As Françoise Vergès writes:

> In *Black Skin, White Masks*'s [sic] footnotes, Fanon often engages himself in a conversation with an imagined opponent or appeals to personal memories and thus reveals more about his thoughts than he does in the text. Fanon's footnotes are like the repressed, the unconscious foundations of his text. Or, in the words of Gayatri Spivak, they are the marginalia of Fanon's text, his way of separating his public from his private self.[25]

---

[23] Ibid., 13.
[24] Ibid., 229.
[25] Françoise Vergès, 'Creole Skin, Black Mask: Fanon and Disavowal,' *Critical Inquiry* 23, no. 3 (Spring 1997), 581-2.

However, if the footnotes are a gesture to separation, this separation is a failure: the private constantly invades the public, which may explain why his earliest work has come to eclipse his later, apparently more famous and more public books. It may be an error, as Vergès argues elsewhere,[26] to call Fanon a psychoanalyst or phenomenologist, as he was a clinical psychiatrist who elaborated much of his anti-colonialism in that context. However, such an insistence reduces any appropriation of Fanon to the status of mere error, which is a serious misunderstanding. In *bricoleur* fashion, Fanon's first book drops certain approaches as it reaches their apparent limits, before returning to them at later moments. Unwilling to confine itself within a single mode of theorising, the text is hybrid and impure. This formal mix destabilises claims to authoritative narrative form, specifically historical narratives expressed in universalist discourses that exclude the question of race. Certainly Fanon states the central question of the text in terms of a narrative of self-consciousness that tends toward primitivist exclusion. I have already quoted part of the following:

> The problem considered here is one of time. Those Negroes and white men will be disalienated who refuse to let themselves be sealed away in the materialized Tower of the Past. For many other Negroes, in other ways, disalienation will come into being through their refusal to accept the present as definitive.[27]

Fanon's text enacts the breaking free from such alienation, in its persistent autobiographical and stylistic invention. It is an example of subjective representation of the problem, which is both a choice for Fanon and a necessity. He writes, 'I have not wished to be objective. Besides, that would be dishonest:

---

[26] Françoise Vergès, 'To Cure and to Free,' in *Fanon: A Critical Reader*, Lewis R. Gordon, T. Denean Sharpley-Whiting and Renée T. White (eds) (Oxford: Blackwell, 1996), 85-99.

[27] Fanon, *Black Skin, White Masks*, 226.

It is not possible for me to be objective.'[28] *Black Skin, White Masks* formally explores and produces the kind of resistance to premature colour-blind universalization it thematically states. This resistance can be formalized in the following way – idealization always takes the form of the purging of a 'black' contingency, so that realization of consciousness for the black (man) always takes the form of being *as if he was white*. Fanon proposes this idealization as the form of relationship between the Antillean male and France, and identifies it as cause of various manifestations of psychiatric illness. He identifies the moment of non-recognition famously at the beginning of 'The Fact of Blackness'; rather, it is a moment at which, 'The black man has no ontological resistance in the eyes of the white man.'[29] Universalization passes over this moment of epidermalization, in which the white gaze fixes the black, in fact:

> I move slowly in the world, accustomed now to seek no longer for upheaval. I progress by crawling. And already I am being dissected under white eyes, the only real eyes. I am *fixed*. Having adjusted their microtomes, they objectively cut away slices of my reality. I am laid bare. I feel, I see in those white faces that it is not a new man who has come in, but a new kind of man, a new genus. Why, it's a Negro![30]

Fanon attends to these moments, insisting on dwelling within them and working through them, before any possible realization of a universal humanity. Of course this insistence is because the *telos* of idealization, in its narrative of developing self-consciousness, is the white (sometimes European) identity. In Fanon's understanding, the humanist reading of Hegelianism implies whiteness as its Absolute. One historical narrative (Hegel's notorious movement from East to West) is

[28] Ibid., 86.
[29] Ibid., 110.
[30] Ibid., 116.

replaced by another, ostensibly more correct, but one which refuses to think the complicity between its colour-blindness and racialized thought. Fanon implies that we should resist the urge to replace this narrative with yet another, at least for the present. So, for Fanon, there is a need to arrest the dialectic in its present form of the irresistible movement toward whiteness, an assimilation masking real and continuing inequalities:

> The dialectic that brings necessity into the foundation of my freedom drives me out of myself. It shatters my unreflected position. Still in terms of consciousness, black consciousness is immanent in its own eyes. I am not a potentiality of something, I am wholly what I am. I do not have to look for the universal. No probability has any place inside me. My Negro consciousness does not hold itself out as a lack. It *is*. It is its own follower.[31]

Of course, Fanon acknowledges that a certain level of totalization is necessary, but argues that it ignores important questions: 'In the beginning I wanted to confine myself to the Antilles. But, regardless of the consequences, dialectic took the upper hand and I was compelled to *see* that the Antillean is first of all a Negro.'[32] It is clear that this emphasis is a question of strategy, and not one of absolute and final identity. In the context of race it is a question of the field of vision, as he indicates in this passage: he is made to see blackness as the necessary point of departure for his analysis. So, as critics have frequently pointed out, Fanon does continually attempt to hold on to distinctions (between different islands, for instance), but at the same time these distinctions are overridden by the outlines of a (finite) theory of racialized colonialist thinking. In a related manner, Fanon reads Sartre's analysis of anti-Semitism, but admits that the assimilation of anti-Semitism to 'negrophobia' appears to be a dangerous totalization, on its way to a grand theory of racism that neglects differences. He then justifies this totalization in

---

[31] Ibid., 135.
[32] Ibid., 172.

terms of the book's intervention in a contemporary crisis, in terms of its strategic potential.

The sense of what distinguishes *Black Skin, White Masks* is sharpened by comparison with *The Wretched of the Earth*. Within the context of the earlier, autobiographically irruptive text, Fanon's analysis of the Antillean male is brutal: the colonial relationship with France, he suggests, has reduced the Antillean male to the level of mere mimicry and impotence. In the earlier text the liberation from this state is an uncertain, anxious endeavour; *The Wretched of the Earth*, by contrast, represents the Algerian male as a pure embodiment of that liberation. The necessity of violence in the Algerian struggle emphasizes a revolutionary purity that is not possible in the argument of the earlier text; indeed, for Sartre in his preface, this is what distinguishes *The Wretched of the Earth*.[33] The Algerian male is not defined by psychological need for the colonizer; in fact, the later text makes direct connections between revolution and psychological cure. However, this figure functions as an idealized representation of the active decolonizing man, and this kind of idealizing elevation of 'action' or 'active forces' is precisely what is put in question by the close of chapter seven in the earlier work, where 'man' is understood as both *yes* and *no*. Early Fanon acknowledges a problematic understanding of action and reaction in Nietzsche, but such circumspection is cast aside in *The Wretched of the Earth*: by contrast with the earlier hesitancy, the later text replaces the old French colonial narrative, compromised by its racist exclusions, with revolutionary chronology. It steps outside what it wishes to oppose, proposing a kind of primitivism: 'Going back to your own people means to become a dirty wog, to go native as much as you can, to become unrecognizable, and to cut off those wings that before you had allowed to grow.'[34] *The Wretched of*

---

[33] Frantz Fanon, *The Wretched of the Earth*, trans. Constance Farrington (New York: Grove Press, 1961), 18.

[34] Ibid., 221.

the Earth steps outside European thought, whilst necessarily subscribing to a form of Marxism. However, the text makes this break through a teleology that installs a 'racist' myth at its origin, in the hope of breaking utterly with that which it despises. The Manichean dialectic found in the later work, proper to its context, is very different from the ambivalence of *Black Skin, White Masks*. However, postcolonial contexts are usually marked by far less definition and certainty, and postcolonial theory is one consequence of this contextual change. Indeed, it is unsurprising that the postcolonial re-evaluation of Fanon was prompted not by the re-reading of *The Wretched of the Earth*, but instead the autobiographical eloquence and uncertainty characterizing *Black Skin, White Masks*.

Thinking about *Black Skin, White Masks* in this way clarifies the formal comparison between Fanon and Marechera. For example, numerous moments of orality in Fanon have their counterparts in Marechera.[35] Like Fanon, Marechera is intent on being autobiographical through *embodiment*. However, the kind of assumptions typically made about a specifically cultural-political embodiment do not interest him: indeed, they are one of the targets of his satire. As Henri Lopes suggests, Marechera is one of many writers seeking 'to enhance identities that are in danger of becoming fossilized in a provincial spirit.'[36] However, this enhancement cannot be through creating newer identities that fulfil the same formal requirements as these fossilized identities. For example, if we take Marechera seriously, it would appear that such identities must not be deep identities. If nothing else, Marechera has a fascination for the superficial, as we see throughout *The Black Insider*. Much of his discussion of this superficiality alludes to semiotic approaches, and a kind of depthlessness that would have been quite in keeping

---

[35] See Maurice Taonezvi Vambe, 'Orality in the Black Zimbabwean Novel in English,' *Journal of Southern African Studies* 30, no. 2 (June 2004), 235-49.
[36] Henri Lopes, 'My Novels, My Characters, and Myself,' *Research in African Literatures* 24, no. 1 (Spring 1993), 85.

with, for example, the Barthes so entranced by his own idea of Japan. Marechera writes in *The Black Insider*, 'My studies have made me my own jester. I cannot say a thing without striking an attitude… Everything is an attitude, a sign. Utterly without depth. Even what we mean is an attitude' (50). This superficiality appears to be opposed to an embodied politics, or at least a straightforward one. Elsewhere there is hostility to any assertion of rootedness, again uneasily fitting embodiment:

> Becoming attitudes; becoming all surface, with no depth under-neath. At the same time, why stress depth, or rootedness for that matter. We are a continent of refugees; one day here, another day there; so much fodder for the boundary makers. There is no sense of home any more, no feeling of being at one with any specific portion of the earth. As you said we have to seek unborn routes and these, like the evidence of ourselves, are yet to come. (108)

Here Africa itself is imagined as being in a state of permanent exile, although, as will be discussed later, the category of exile is problematic when made metaphorical. In any case, if there is going to be an 'African Image,' it has to be one from the future: it cannot be 'evidence of ourselves' derived from a mythical past. It can be suggested, after Derrida, that this evidence must be spectral, or must always remain *to-come*. Such sentiments are difficult to square with identity politics and, throughout, the book puts such politics in question. The emperor's new clothes becomes a constant point of reference, with Marechera concerned to defend personality from the demands of identity politics:

> The idea of personality molded by the cultural artifacts outside us and the sense of identity with a specific time and place, as though the human being is as rooted in his own kind of soil as any weed, is what creates for us the emperor's new clothes. And it is quite easy inflexibly to deceive ourselves that we are fully clothed and not naked. (110-11)

This critical demand that identity retain a flexibility toward the individual fits well Marechera's concerns about the 'African Image,' but is something picked up in various other contexts throughout the book. For example, there is the following judgment on genetics, which is reminiscent of Fanon's *scientistic* language in his dissection of racist objectivity: 'a cold and chilling engineering which would deny us uniqueness' (119). Then, there is the conclusion about getting involved in the real Africa, rather than staying locked inside one's uniqueness: 'Man, if that's what reality is, then I'm all right, Jack, locked up inside my own head' (124). Of course, as in the sections recalling racism in Britain, Marechera is clear that others will not allow you to remain locked inside your own conception of identity and self-worth. Nonetheless, here *The Black Insider* plays with a refusal of becoming, of dialectical movements of identity depending on interaction with others. The scrubbing figure conjured up in 'Black Skin What Mask,' desperately trying to deny the body, is one possible consequence of getting involved in the world: the world will demand one thing or another from you, and will try positively or negatively to impose its idea of your identity. More than that, you will try to assume that identity, however empty the identity may be. Remember the question addressed to the novelist, about the category of African writer into which he falls: 'Are you angry and polemic or are you grim and nocturnal or are you realistic and quavering or are you indifferent and European?' (168). The questioner reflects that those are the categories, so far as she remembers, as if indeed there might be a list written down somewhere.

Which brings us to the question of the writer. Pattison has suggested that this question is central to understanding the book; he writes of, 'the definitive theme of *The Black Insider*: Marechera's journey to become a writer.'[37] It is certainly the case that all the various characters are not only facets of Marechera,

---

[37] Pattison, 'Call No Man Happy,' 223.

but also indications of the stages of a writer's struggle. Then there are various metafictional discussions that take place, not to mention a dismissive perspective on the supposedly democratic possibilities of the writing process. To understand the place of the writer, I want to focus on a specific reference to a form that may seem marginal to understanding Marechera – the aphorism. Much of what has been argued so far can also be understood in terms of aphoristic speech. It is important to remember the debates found in *The Black Insider* about the suitability of the novel form. Critics have written perceptively on Marechera's carnivalesque, and he himself of course provided numerous clues for this reading, both in the literary works themselves and in marginal texts. The aphorism, however, appears to be a useful category for understanding just what is so striking about his work: the individual sentence level is where some of his most obvious effects are achieved, and individual sentences demand interpretive effort in themselves. Indeed, at one point we read that, 'Every man is a walking collection of aphorisms. The thing about a story lurking around every corner, and a novel resting uneasily inside every human skull. Nonsense' (123). Derrida himself has written suggestively on aphorisms, but the thinker I wish to introduce here is Gilles Deleuze, who writes of Nietzsche in terms of both aphorism and the irresponsible, so bringing us close to Marechera.

Deleuze declares at one point: 'Irresponsibility – Nietzsche's most noble and beautiful secret.'[38] When Deleuze places emphasis on the aphorism as suited to Nietzsche's purpose because it explicitly requires evaluation, he does so in a text that strains between the dutiful explication (being) and the semi-aphoristic (becoming). Certain texts cannot remain within the terms of formalization if they are not to appear deaf to their own propositions, which is why Fanon writes as he writes, and of course is what we expect from Marechera,

[38] Gilles Deleuze, *Nietzsche and Philosophy*, trans. Hugh Tomlinson (London: Athlone Press, 1983), 9.

despite his works not being theory at all. Aphorism announces the other, constitutes the other, is a foreign language; but translation has always begun prior to any empirical instance of translation of thought or language. This structure characterizes much of Nietzsche's work too, and helps us understand the irresponsibility that we find in Marechera. As China Miéville has suggested, there is a necessary engagement with the aphoristic in reading Marechera:

> He demands sustained effort from the reader, so that the work is almost interactive-reading it is an active process of collaboration with the writer – and the metaphors are simultaneously so unclichéd and so apt that he reinvigorates the language.[39]

This kind of participation is exactly what Barthes, of course, finds valuable in certain kinds of literature, but is also what he tries to achieve in his critical work, which is no doubt why he appeals to Marechera. Indeed, *Black Skin, White Masks* could also be understood in this way, as demanding participation rather than being, as Barthes has put it, accepted or rejected by referendum.[40] However much he may proclaim that he is locked inside his own head, Marechera's reader finds him wandering the streets, becoming engaged, and being responsible.

Analysis of postcolonial life-writing often overlaps with discussions of exile and its apparent privilege in postcolonial cultural analysis. For example, in discussing Edward Said's autobiographical works, it is very difficult to ignore his numerous reflections on exile. But of course the category and experience of exile are both contentious. Kenneth Parker notes that the postcolonial era led to forms of exile that produced the figure of 'the writer as casualty.'[41] Unsurprisingly, one of

---

[39] Joan Gordon, 'Reveling in Genre: An Interview with China Miéville,' *Science Fiction Studies* 30, no. 3 (November 2003), 359.

[40] Roland Barthes, *S/Z: An Essay*, trans. Richard Miller (New York: Hill and Wang, 1974), 4.

[41] Kenneth Parker, 'Home is Where the Heart...Lies,' *Transition* 59 (1993), 66.

his examples is Marechera. Parker is discussing, amongst other things, Timothy Brennan's critique of metropolitan cosmo-politan writers, privileged as interpreters of their 'homelands,' although rejected by the rules of those often newly indepen-dent nations. Parker thinks it disturbing that Brennan should make common cause with these rulers, who of course desired control over the representation of their 'experiments' in inde-pendence. It is certainly the case that criticisms of exile as such, in wanting to distinguish 'real' from 'upwardly-mobile' exile, can slip into easy *ad hominem* attacks. When it comes to Marechera, his forensic eye mercilessly picked over the question of his own exile, as is evident at many points in *The Black Insider*: 'Let those who will, cool their heels in London' (57). In any case, even if we did not have the ever-present specter of Marechera's life to remind us of certain brutal realities, in his work it seems impossible to find any real privilege in being an exile; indeed, Paul Zeleza refers to Marechera's 'exilic despair.'[42] The episodes of life led in Oxford and London are evidence of the impossibility of living inside one's own mind, secure in one's individuality: everywhere others demand you fit their idea or image of a communal but not plural identity, racist or not.

Of course, being required to depart from the security of one's own mind has more than one meaning. On the one hand, there is the usual skepticism if not cynicism about the African Image, as found for example in the remark that, 'it was in our interest to appear united' (91). On the other hand, there is an acknowledgement that criticism of community comes at a price. At one point, Marechera writes the following: 'This was the tearing cloth of exile, and of the sense of being in a world in which one yearned to leap out of one's mind' (84). This yearning is the exile's need for community, for belonging, a yearning that exists despite Marechera's usual desire for

---

[42] Paul Tiyambe Zeleza, 'The Politics and Poetics of Exile: Edward Said in Africa,' *Research in African Literatures* 36, no. 3 (Autumn 2005), 17.

what Derrida calls participation without belonging. 'Exile in London,' Marechera proclaims, 'is so demoralizing. You're all changed. You all don't come on like you used to do back home. I mean everyone looks phoney and suspicious and cynical and there's no black feeling among us any more' (85). Lacking community, one also lacks individuality, at least any authentic individuality worth the name. The text's numerous references to forms of role play are again ambivalent. At one point, he writes that, 'I really was enjoying playing the role of the unfathomable black intellectual mind. I still do' (87). But of course that is not the only role he plays, just as his texts do not retain a formal or generic consistency for any length of time. Just as in Fanon's great work of autobiographical theory, *The Black Insider* fragments in order to resist a dialectical gathering-up into a coherent, broad, communal identity. However, this resistance is not a resistance to community as such. The stress on surface at the expense of depth can be a kind of postmodern tic, but it is also something that Marechera does not embrace wholeheartedly or simplistically.

Accordingly, it appears that the kind of artificiality ascribed to the 'African Image' is not so far away from the superficiality inherent in and required for every constantly mutating individual identity. On the African Image, Marechera writes:

> Having built its existence on a denial of Victorian psycho-anthro-pology, on a denial of race and cultural inferiority, it could only sustain itself by continued denial. But how long would the provocation last? If it was suddenly withdrawn, someone would have to invent it again. (90)

However, invention is not a straightforwardly negative phenomenon, and artificiality can come in many forms. Recollecting London's Africa Centre, he writes that, 'Here then was the womb into which one could retreat to nibble at the warm fluids of an Africa that would never be anything other than artificial' (91). The problem with this kind of artificiality is *not* that it is artificial as such, but that it plunges into what Fanon calls a 'black hole:' it is closed-off, a mystification of African identity. If there is going to be an African identity, it must be a leap into the future.

In this way, Marechera and Fanon share a difficult stress on what Derrida would call the *future to-come*. Marechera expresses this difficult thought in thematic terms that could also be applied to textual form: 'I am only complete when I feel something's missing; something unattainable, like a purpose, a design' (101). To return to an earlier quotation; like Fanon, Marechera writes in the belief that 'we have to seek unborn routes and these, like the evidence of ourselves, are yet to come' (108). Like Fanon, for Marechera this evidence will always be 'to come,' but that should not be taken to mean that their work is apolitical, although clearly with Marechera there are strains of resistance to political utility narrowly conceived. Instead, the leaps into the future entailed by their work will be made without guarantees.

7 The Avant-Garde Power of *Black Sunlight*
Radical Recontextualizations of Marechera from Darius James to China Miéville

MARK P. WILLIAMS

This chapter is about the radicalism of avant-garde writing under globalization. It links the writing of British Marxist fantasy novelist China Miéville and African-American performance artist Darius James with Dambudzo Marechera's novel *Black Sunlight*, which both authors have named as a specific influence. It does so in order to explore the capacity of literature to reflect upon the politics of globalization and initiate dissent. My argument follows on from Michael Hardt and Antonio Negri in *Empire*,[1] which argues that the culture of postmodernity and the economic system of the world market mutually support one another, constituting the dominant ideology of globalization.

For Hardt and Negri, Empire is a new social formation which takes the whole world as its territory; a system which allows multiple meta-narratives to interpenetrate and co-exist by regulating and managing the ideological conflicts of workers and interest groups economically and socially. It does this economically by differentiating blocks, regions, nations and locales, and sectors such as public and private, within the overarching world market, and socially by differentiating nationalities, ethnicities, regional, gendered and sexual identities, and political affiliations, within an overarching global culture of postmodernity.

Empire argues that this system favors particular economic regions directly at the expense of others by reproducing the economic conditions which enrich more dominant nations and impoverish less dominant ones, simultaneously reproducing

[1] Michael Hardt and Antonio Negri, *Empire* (Cambridge, MA: Harvard UP, 2000).

cultural forms which naturalize these economic conditions as logical consequences of globalized trade. Drawing on Guy Debord and the Situationist International, Hardt and Negri term this ideological naturalizing mechanism the spectacular society.[2] Spectacular society is a media culture which lays claim to a uniquely authentic representative function for accessing the Real, extending from global news and entertainment to all cultural and artistic forms by managing and differentiating international markets for cultural products such as art and literature.

In attempting to formulate ways this complex network can be untangled by the subjects constituted within it, Hardt and Negri propose that modes of resistance must attack the foundational assumptions of Empire (the naturalization of the world markets and of global media) at all possible levels simultaneously; they write that 'Empire cannot be resisted by a project aimed at a limited, local autonom … we must push through Empire to come out the other side;' they propose that 'Globalization must be met with a counter-globalization, Empire with a counter-Empire.'[3] To them, the key problem is to find imaginative techniques for connecting the individual with the seemingly diffuse spaces of globalization in a concrete way, a project that requires simultaneously abstracting cultural activities from their local or generic (managed, differentiated) contexts to see them in light of their place within postmodernity, grasping how they reproduce the conditions of Empire:

> The very qualitites of labour power (difference, measure and determination) can no longer be grasped, and similarly, exploitation can no longer be localized and quantified. In effect the object of exploitation and domination tend not to be specific productive activities but the universal capacity to produce, that is, abstract social activity and its comprehensive power.[4]

---

[2] See Guy Debord, *The Society of The Spectacle*, trans. Donald Nicholson Smith (New York: Zone Books, 1995).

[3] Hardt and Negri, *Empire*, 206-7.

[4] Ibid., 204.

To develop a comprehensive aesthetic vision capable of expressing these problems in art and culture requires an approach to specific arts and cultural forms which locates them within the linkages of globalization and challenges their situation. For Hardt and Negri, the true literature of globalization is a counter literature, resisting the capacity of literature to maintain the system which differentiates and manages it culturally into its diverse national and regional traditions and into market-driven genres.

This chapter will explore the ability of Marechera's fiction to function as a counter-literature within globalization by comparing *Black Sunlight* counter-contextually with works from traditions and canons that would otherwise be separate within the world market for literatures in English, but whose authors have encountered Marechera's text through that market and found it significant and resonant with their own interests: Darius James' *Negrophobia: An Urban Parable* (1992) and China Miéville's *The Scar* (2002). In connecting the otherwise very different writers Miéville and James through their thematic overlaps with Marechera, I want to propose a conceptualization of Marechera's work as an aesthetic resistance to the differentiation, assimilation, and management of subjectivities of globalization's dominant ideology.

I argue that the importance of Marechera's work for reading literature in respect to globalization is that it openly invites such transverse readings across multiple literatures and cultural traditions. It is internationalist and avant-garde. The strength of the avant-garde lies precisely in its ability to bridge the divides (conventional forms and publishing conventions) which separate texts such as *Black Sunlight*, *Negrophobia*, and *The Scar* into their relative (anti-)canons. This chapter proposes no counter-canon. It merely reads to establish new grounds on which to base our evaluation of texts.

Dambudzo Marechera's writing famously resists categorization, as commentators such as Annie Gagiano have observed. In her essay on 'Marecheran Postmodernism,' she describes

Marechera as being simultaneously 'considered too European for Africa and too African for Europe.'[5] The work of Marechera, then, is almost a gesture in defiance of genre expectation in itself since Marechera's own use of dense allusion and confrontational imagery do not merely upset readerly expectations but have upset many different readers; his works are idiosyncratic and infused with an anarchic sensibility that extended to his private life.[6] All of his fictions, from *Guardian* Prize-winning *The House of Hunger*, to *The Black Insider*, and the collection *Scrapiron Blues*, are resistant to conventions both literary and social. He favors Modernism and Surrealism, counter to the taste of Chinua Achebe, the founding editor of the African Writers Series which published *Black Sunlight*. The subject-matter of his stories has provoked as much censure as praise for being, variously, Eurocentric, obscene and, of course, politically contentious.

Marechera's *Black Sunlight* begins and ends with alienated subjectivity attempting to grasp its place in a world emerging from colonial domination into neo-liberal economic and cultural domination, what Hardt and Negri categorize as the step from postcolonial modernity to postmodernity.[7] At the beginning of the text, alienation is presented as the product of the estranged mind-state of the protagonist, Christian, a photo-journalist, who has returned from Oxford to find his home country – seemingly the whole of Africa – undergoing civil strife. The text, then, presents itself as a novel which will ultimately conform to a model of Social Realism inflected by the Modernist tradition where estranged prose is the result of the alienated subjectivity of characters. In fact, this is a masquerade. The underlying structure of the novel actually poses the question of whether modeling subjectivity by ideological means and expressing subjectivity under ideology can ever be separated into cause

---

[5] Gagiano, Annie. 'Marecheran Postmodernism: Mocking the Bad Joke of "African Modernity".' *Journal of Literary Studies* 18, no. 1 (2002), 70.

[6] Kirsten Holst Petersen, *An Articulate Anger: Dambudzo Marechera, 1952–87* (Sydney: Dangaroo Press, 1988).

[7] Hardt and Negri, *Empire*, 139–46.

and effect. Marechera's protagonist meets his double, a writer, who tells him 'I have been in this room for as long as I can remember inventing you from the first page of that manuscript' before questioning whether this relationship might be reversed: suggesting that perhaps Christian has 'been out there for as long as you can remember inventing me up to this point.'[8] Similar reversals of attention to textual conventions, questioning the relationship between form and content, are present in both *Negrophobia* and *The Scar* in ways that resonate powerfully with Marechera when considered in relation to the place of literature as a global market. The diversity of James' and Miéville's cultural contexts only serves to accentuate the significance of the common thematic echoes between them and Marechera.

The work of Darius James emerges from the specific cultural milieu of the post-1970s Lower East Side of New York, a significant and influential arts scene.[9] James' interests are broad in scope and cultural engagement, dealing with race, gender and sexuality, reflecting an internationalist perspective. *Negrophobia: An Urban Parable*, his most famous text, is written as a screenplay for an unfilmable phantasmagoric film, the ultimate in Blaxploitation satire, tackling race, gender, and sexuality in a dizzyingly complex array of Swiftian vignettes. An intellectual context for this work must necessarily include mention of his association with a highly diverse group of writers with avantgarde interests. These range from notable members of the Umbra Workshop, later the core of the Black Arts Movement, such as Steve Cannon to writers such as Dennis Cooper and Joel Rose, whose work blends multiple popular idioms such as crime novel and 'street' fictions with postmodernist textual strategies. James also signals support and affection for the work of TV satirist Michael O'Donoghue and British post-punk avant-gardist Stewart Home.

---

8   Dambudzo Marechera, *Black Sunlight* (London: Heinemann, 1980), 62.
9   Lorenzo Thomas, 'Alea's Children: The Avant-Garde on the Lower East Side, 1960-1970,' *African American Review* 27, no. 4 (Winter, 1993), 573–8.

Equally, the intellectual contemporaries of James identified by academics form a complex mixture. In the 'Call for Papers' for a special issue of the *African American Review*, Bertram D. Ashe identifies James with what he terms the 'Post-Soul Aesthetic,' welcoming comparison between a list of artists, performers, musicians, writers and filmmakers that also includes: Jean-Michel Basquiat, Dave Chappelle, Mos Def, The Roots, Me'Shell Ndege-Ocello, Paul Beatty and Spike Lee. On James' web-page, Ashe lists a great number of other texts and writers whose work interests him and intersects with his own, including prominent figures characterized as 'avant-garde' such as Kathy Acker and William S. Burroughs. It is in this list, sandwiched between 'the works of Michael O'Donoghue' and 'Abbie Hofman's *Revolution for the Hell of It,*' that he refers to Dambudzo Marechera's *Black Sunlight*.

As a specific text, *Black Sunlight* has many resonances with *Negrophobia* – both use estrangement techniques; both employ dense literary and cultural allusion to foreground textuality and the construction of narrative perception as a form of dissimulation; both play with the cyclical form of the dream-vision text; and both employ visual metaphors and the concept of reflection to thematically link these concerns at key points. More importantly, both *Negrophobia* and *Black Sunlight* open with framing devices which foreground their status as textual objects and highlight the same problem of cultural perception through abstract images. Subjectivity is at the core of these texts, and although the cultural context of Miéville's *The Scar* appears to be quite different, presenting very different resonances with *Black Sunlight*, upon exploration these texts seem to circle around the same debates.

China Miéville draws intellectually on a tradition of British Marxism and its associated history of educated working-class dissent, and aesthetically on a post-New Wave science fiction and fantasy tradition in the UK. The British New Wave was inflected by European avant-garde modes such as Brechtian theatre and Surrealism. It was formed by writers associated with *New Worlds SF* magazine in the 1960s as edited by Michael Moorcock, such as the notable UK writers Brian Aldiss and J.G. Ballard; the American authors Samuel R. Delany and Norman Spinrad; those who were to edit later issues, such as Hilary Bailey and Charles Platt; and those emerging writers such as M. John Harrison who in fact became the first Books Editor of *New Worlds*. Their radical overhaul of style and content in British science fiction and fantasy strongly affected the work of subsequent generations of novelists.[10] This heritage in contemporary fantasy has been identified by a variety of practitioners as the 'New Weird,' a term which links it both to 'New Wave' science fiction and to the early-twentieth century pulp traditions of Weird fiction associated with writers like William Hope Hodgson and H.P. Lovecraft.[11] Understood very broadly, New Weird is a kind of urban fantasy which engages with postmodernity through surrealist imagery.

Miéville's version of the New Weird employs surrealist disjuncture within his fantasy world to open up spaces which provoke allegorical (meta-)readings of his settings, characters, creatures and plots while eschewing metafictional distance from the fantastic. As such, it operates as a kind of secular visionary mode. In this way, Miéville makes use of surrealist resistance to form within the formal conventions of fantasy novels. In *The Scar*, the dominant formal convention is the quest narrative; in *Negrophobia*, it is the screenplay. In *Black Sunlight* the dominant formal convention is the social realist novel. Importantly, the deep structures of all these texts partake in a debate which is central to the avant-garde – the representation of postmodernity as a political engagement in the world.

[10] See Colin Greenland, *The Entropy Exhibition: Michael Moorcock and the UK 'New Wave'* (London: Routledge & Kegan Paul, 1983); Brian Aldiss and David Wingrove, *Trillion Year Spree: The History of Science Fiction* (London: Victor Gollancz, 1986); and, Adam Roberts, *The History of Science Fiction* (Basingstoke: Palgrave Macmillan, 2007).

[11] Jeff VanderMeer and Ann VanderMeeer, eds, *The New Weird* (San Francisco: Tachyon, 2008).

The notion of avant-garde representation is itself a challenge. To the extent that it is possible to formulate a sense of what might be meant by an artistic/literary avant-garde at any point in history, the term 'avant-garde' must be understood as contingent and historically determined. The avant-garde is an aesthetic concerned with negation – the avant-garde *is not*, that is, it is primarily understood as resistance to what *is* in the realm of the contemporary aesthetic. Clive Bloom writes that 'Avant-garde intellectual thought is always constituted by its antagonism to the present regimes of thought … to bring into being the regime of the future.'[12] Where there are art traditions the avant-garde will respond with anti-art, responding to anti-art. But, it will also respond to anti-art with new art, and so on. The point is that the avant-garde must always be oppositional, resistant, and progressive in its attempt to overcome present conditions in its incessant push for betterment.

I take the perspective that the principles of avant-garde art and literature formulate a political critique of the means of artistic and literary production through two primary strategies: redirection of content and attack on form. Both strategies demonstrate the linkages between artistic and literary production in the present regimes of ideology and attempt to negate them by first exposing them. The creative decision as to whether redirection of content or attack on form constitutes the more effective method for generating a critique of ideology can be considered as a concretization of the ethical dimension of art and literature. For the purposes of my discussion here, I will consider two main technical strands: *the anarchic*, which is concerned with techniques which promote the free play of meaning; and *the didactic*, which is concerned with techniques which promote the critical application of practice to controlling meanings. Importantly, though, both of these are employed together in differing combinations in order to variously invite

---

[12] Clive Bloom, *Literature, Politics and Intellectual Crisis in Britain Today* (Basingstoke: Palgrave MacMillan, 2001), 147.

or resist the possibilities of counter-readings even with the understanding that counter-readings may exist, but the text's relationship to them will always vary.

Limited to a discussion of novelistic fiction, these techniques tend towards producing, on the one hand, politically tendentious novels, utilizing combinations of established and successful aesthetic forms (conventions) which convey resistant content by dramatizing political positions, and, on the other, anti-novels which attack the aesthetic forms themselves as complicit in, or being manifestations of, the dominant ideology. It is possible to suggest a degree of correspondence between Miéville's fantasy novel *The Scar* with the use of established form, and Darius James' *Negrophobia* with the attack on form. In this schema, Marechera's *Black Sunlight* presents us with an ideal third term unifying the other two, providing an aesthetic bridge between them. However, this construction elides the degree to which the two technical strands not only co-exist within any given text, but perhaps necessarily function co-dependently within avant-garde writing in general.

The ideal third term, a unification of anarchic freedom and controlled direction as twin negations of existing practice, is in many respects the point of highest critical insight implied by the concept of the avant-garde. This conception of a third term where critical insight and aesthetic practice are simultaneously optimal is particularly important to the Surrealist movement.[13] According to Michael Richardson and Krzysztof Fijalkowski, Surrealism is 'proteiform, defined not by what it is but what it will become ... the will to discover that point at which opposing categories are no longer perceived contradictorily (the "supreme point").'[14] This 'supreme point' is always limited by historical circumstance and must be subject to continuous renewal. The play on the *limitations* of avant-garde texts' ability

---

[13] J.H. Matthews, *The Surrealist Mind* (London: Associated UP, 1991), 24-30.
[14] Michael Richardson and Krzystof Fijalkowski (eds), *Surrealism Against The Current* (London: Pluto Press, 2001), 6.

to utilize and attack formal convention is essential to their successful functioning as radical texts. The avant-garde must subvert itself in order to really make a difference. The sense of continuous renewal which this implies is crucial to the three texts under discussion here. *Black Sunlight*, *Negrophobia*, and *The Scar* all articulate a demand for the renewal of perception by playing with the imaginary and symbolic in creating the worlds of their fictions. Indeed, they all place a strong emphasis on textuality and offer parallel critical insights on the relationship of *character* and *reader* perception. In this way, they thematically engage with their own limitations as texts within their form and within the nebulous, but powerful, global media culture of postmodernity.

Their contexts could not seem more different, but the locus of all three texts is the non-space of postmodernity as a force which overarches all contexts of cultural expression. *Black Sunlight* opens and closes with a prose-poetic tirade which seems to attack the very possibility of representation, simultaneously denying and affirming the 'reality' of the events which the book will contain. The opening lines, which arrive before we know their provenance, are particularly suggestive:

> Within this pale womb with its beard, a brutal story writhes … Through the open window, blows the slashing winds. From a long ago, astonishment comes. From a once upon a time, that fucking window of fiction, astonishment comes.[15]

'Astonishment' refers both to a character's astonishment and also to the more abstract sense of a story producing astonishment in its reader by the kind of defamiliarization these opening lines represent. The words relate both the estranged mind state of the narratorial voice, resolved into the narrator Christian, and the textual estrangement which Marechera, as author, is couching his narrative so that the novel begins with an anarchic play of

---

[15] Marechera, *Black Sunlight*, 1.

meaning and becomes structured into a more didactic, social realist-based mode.

Christian has been chased, beaten and imprisoned, a defamiliarized perspective could be said to express this violence; it is common to Marechera's other texts such as 'House of Hunger' where the details of a story are deliberately confused with the act of writing by a narrator-character – 'Love and hate or the desire for revenge are just so many stains on a sheet, on a wall, on a page even. This page.'[16] However, *Black Sunlight* begins from a position which might be conceptualized as the 'thoughts' of abstract narrative attempting to produce itself by becoming 'character' and 'events.' As the novel progresses this abstraction becomes tied to the character Christian but as it concludes it becomes partly freed from this constraint again, becoming text-as-text once more; and the anarchic free play of meaning stages a return. This ambiguous relationship with representation is echoed in *Negrophobia* and *The Scar*.

Darius James' choice of narrative strategy in *Negrophobia* forces the reader to consider the relationship between signifier and referent by ironically denying the novel's textual status. Utilizing the conventions of the screenplay it leads its audience to an internalization of counter-reading: although published as a novel, every detail of the text pretends to be something other in its form. It begins with filmic instructions to 'OPEN ON' the 'INT' of a 'Brownstone in Manhattan's Upper West Side,' and an 'EXTREME CLOSE-UP OF A JOINT:'

The camera follows the joint's curling, serpentine ribbons of smoke in a slow upward tilt. The shot is held in midair as the gathering curls of smoke form the title in exotic lettering:

NEGROPHOBIA
The title dissipates in the darkness. Dolly through smoke and gloom. Stop on a pair of charred, sequined Come-Fuck-Me Shoes hanging at the end of a ribbon draped over a nail.[17]

---

[16] Dambudzo Marechera, *The House of Hunger* (London: Heinemann, 1978), 55.
[17] Darius James, *Negrophobia: An Urban Parable* (New York: Citadel, 1992), 3-4.

This then dissolves into a 'Montage of Polaroid prints' of 'pudding-soft PUBESCENTS' with 'bosoms bobbing under swastika-emblazoned valentine Ts' who turn out to be vampires; it is the reader's introduction to the world of Bubbles Brazil described as a 'drug-addled teenage girl,' a world of whirling images which the narration demands that the reader accepts as images.[18] The prose seems to offer didactic explanations for its estranged nature – the lead character is 'drug-addled,' it is really a screenplay not a novel, so need not develop novelistically – but the result is actually to distract the reader from their own complicity in accepting the images, a very similar use of form to that of *The Scar*.

Miéville's *The Scar* is set in the fantasy world of Bas Lag. It opens as the protagonist, Bellis Coldwine, leaves her home city-state of New Crobuzon intending to emigrate to the New World, 'Nova Esperium.'[19] Bellis is estranging herself from her familiar environment (familiar, too, to readers of Miéville's previous novel *Perdido Street Station*) to go into hiding. Her ship is hijacked by pirates who assimilate it into the floating city of Armada, opening a narrative didactically concerned with the loss of cultural bearings. The genre conventions which govern the narrative thereafter – fantasy, pirates, high seas adventure, foreign lands, strange creatures, espionage, and a mythical place of infinite possibilities – strongly point towards a quest narrative structure, but Miéville subverts this expectation, presenting instead a more anarchic story of diverse cultural and political battles within the society of Armada. Bellis writes an epistolary narrative of her journey which becomes a major focalizing technique for drawing the reader into her perspective, but Miéville uses this to show the limitations of focusing on a single perspective within a society that is itself in varying relationships with diverse other political interests.

In *Rhetorics of Fantasy*, Farah Mendlesohn argues that Bellis'

---

[18]   Ibid., 4-5.
[19]   China Miéville, *The Scar* (London: Macmillan, 2002), 13.

narrative is an almost precise inversion of the expectations of a quest. The central character not only has little to do with the quest, she is *on the wrong side throughout* since New Crobuzon is the imperialist-expansionist force which is threatening the sovereignty of other cultures.[20] In this way, it can be seen as an attack on the totalizing impulse towards both differentiation and assimilation as strategies for creating dominant metanarratives within globalized exchanges, and as a resistance to the expectations of its audience, similar in that sense to *Negrophobia* and *Black Sunlight*. *The Scar* uses the conventions of the quest narrative in the same way that *Negrophobia* uses the textual conventions of the screenplay and *Black Sunlight* those of social realism – they function as frames which appear to anchor the disjunctures of character, location and imagery but which operate conversely to manipulate the position of the reader, making the reader's relationship with text-as-text a theme of the novel. The texts masquerade the solidity of their textual conventions in order to ultimately draw the reader's attention to the fluidity which underpins their own conventional assumptions about the representation of 'the real.' In this way, perception and ideology are revealed to be the core matter of all three novels.

Neutrality in representation is central to the interrogation of perception staged by all three texts. An important effect of Darius James' screenplay strategy is that it allows him to adopt a voice which appears as neutral, relating directly to the reader events that *they are seeing* on the screen of their imagination. It produces a concretely different effect from the narrative framing of novel-within-a-novel employed by Percival Everett to address similar questions in *Erasure* (2001). Within *Erasure*, the narrator writes a novel titled *My Pafology* (later retitled *Fuck*) to parody the idea of authentic representation in 'street' fictions, making the play between sign and referent recognizably literary. *Negrophobia*, contrastingly,

[20] Farah Mendlesohn, *Rhetorics of Fantasy* (Middletown, CT: Wesleyan UP, 2008), 56-8.

appears self-reflexively anti-literary, written as if it were non-literature, but is crammed with diverse literary allusion, such as meeting an albino called 'Al-Shebop Shabazz Hazred' on the subway, a character whose name combines black Muslim parody and H.P. Lovecraft's stereotypical 'mad Arab' Abdul Al-Hazred, the author of the *Necronomicon*.[21]

Negrophobia's language pretends to be read as though it were purely composed of image, thereby didactically structuring the anarchic disjuncture of its imagery. Further, James gives no narrative framing through the perception of a single character. Despite being focalized around the character of Bubbles Brazil, we are left with the reception of images in equivalence: the images of prejudice are there for the reader to actively project while they are *told* that they are passively viewing them. The grotesques and caricatures we encounter include the Licorice Men, 'tar-colored DWARVES with sagging toadlike skin' (65); Uncle Sambo 'a bug-eyed black man in a stovepipe hat and a star-spangled, red, white and blue striped suit' encountered in the 'Church of Uncle H. Rap Remus' (73); the film-within-the-film called 'The Rocky Horror Negro Show' which ferociously satirizes sacred cows such as Walt Disney, JFK, and Elvis (88-112); and the extraterrestrial being known as Talking Dreads, whose attempts to communicate beneficial insights to humanity have been deformed by the racist consciousness of his chosen 'receptor,' a 'Scottish woman living in India' (124). Talking Dreads complains that his image became 'skewed in her mind, rooted and spread like weed,' manifesting as '*Lil' Black Zambo*' (124). James leaves the reader (as passive viewer) to receive these images and interpret them as if they were simply being bombarded with them visually, accepting their unacceptability. It is James' central narrative subversion, then, that the reader is the screen on which the film 'NEGROPHOBIA' is projected within the novel. This is also the significance of Bellis Coldwine's use of an epistolary narrative to make sense

[21] James, *Negrophobia*, 19.

of her situation in *The Scar*.

Although the reader has access to other characters' inner lives in Miéville's novel, it is only Bellis who *writes* about her experiences, placing herself at the centre of her own narrative and inviting the reader to follow suit as her reader. Indeed, only towards the end of the novel is the reader confronted with the limitations of Bellis' perspective – she is not central to events, she is culturally imperialist, and she is also unconsciously racist. At this point the reader has already been manipulated into sharing her greatest misapprehensions of cultural difference, glossing racial differences based on appearance in terms of Otherness because of the conventions of the quest narrative which calls for 'monsters' and 'fabulous creatures' rather than merely people. The people in question are the inhabitants of The Gengris called the grindylow. Through Bellis, the reader learns that 'the distinction between race and place was unclear' and the grindylow are considered to be 'aquatic daemons or monsters or degenerate crossbred men and women depending on which story one believed.'[22] Bellis thinks of them in terms of an essential alien-ness that leads her to be deceived and manipulated by a fellow passenger from New Crobuzon. As with Marechera's *Black Sunlight* and James' *Negrophobia*, it is through the attitude to representations of difference that cultural prejudices are exposed to critical attention within the framework of postmodernity which supposedly encourages equality by differentiating identities.

These texts problematize the relation of perception to culture through their agonistic engagement with authenticity. This relationship foregrounds the necessary limitation of any partial perspective on the part of the characters and presents a textual equivalent encouraging the reader to regard textual conventions as manipulations of perspective. Only a text which engages with the limitations of fiction while refusing to wholly break faith with its fictional status can represent the place of

[22] Miéville, *The Scar*, 126-7.

both reader and writer within the linkages of postmodernity which surround them – the global market for literature; the attempt to create a didactic narrative is always underpinned by an anarchic slippage between the authentic and inauthentic. *Negrophobia* and *The Scar* share this agonistic approach to culture with *Black Sunlight*. Marechera's protagonist, Christian, makes disjunctive uses of literary language conventions and literary allusion to attempt to understand his own place in his world, acknowledging as he does so that this makes his subjectivity a matter of fiction:

> There are more immediate things in the world than all my travel and Oxford degree. As I fought through a stubborn tangle of ropelike undergrowth, getting scratched, gouged, gagged, entangled, I thought of Sparta and Athens and how the runner got through. I fought thicker and thicker into the mass of thorny vines. I heard running feet. They seemed to come from every side. It was black. I simply stood perfectly still right in the middle of that now – I hoped – blessed hideous undergrowth. They seemed to pass by, those footsteps. I willed my heart to cease its howling beat. I willed my heart of darkness to stop wheezing horror – horror.[23]

The image created by the allusion to Sparta and Athens suggests that the protective core of classical culture functions as a kind of armour to protect against the chaos of the 'savage' (non-Eurocentric) environment, while Christian's name and relationship with European literature suggest both *The Pilgrim's Progress* (1678) and the missionary ideology attendant upon colonialism. In the novel he is a photographic journalist whose compositions double the flat reportage style which accompanies some of the passages describing civil unrest in the novel, doubling Marechera's author function. Where he wills his 'heart of darkness to stop wheezing horror – horror' he wryly takes on the other aspect of this cloak of acculturation:

[23] Marechera, *Black Sunlight*, 9.

the concept that his Oxford degree, his 'literariness,' wears him, indeed, colonizes and manages his embodied subjectivity through perception.

A similar manipulation of authenticity takes place in the scenes of *Negrophobia*, using language borrowed from American underground commix: Bubbles Brazil's school, 'Donald Goines Senior High,' is decorated in 'multicoloured sprays of Vaughn Bodé nymphs' alongside 'posters of Marcus Garvey, Malcolm X, and Bob Marley.'[24] This knowingly overcomplicated backdrop, mixing iconographies of diverse counter cultures, plays host to racial stereotypes 'snorting smack from tiny waxed-paper sacks; drinking pints of Wild Irish Rose; sucking tubes of crack; fighting with razors; firing pistols,' and, even more provocatively, 'miscarrying half-formed fetuses; singing gospel; and wailing the blues' (26). The anarchic density of imagery and the tone of the prose offset one another: the coruscating imagery demands to be read didactically, as Bubbles' own racist perception, while the neutral tone of the screenplay suggests that it is merely reporting to the reader what *they* see. As with the slippage between Social Realist and abstract narrative in *Black Sunlight*, the reader is effectively trapped between textual strategies inviting rejection and acceptance: the text asks in whose imagination these caricatures appear. An unproblematic answer is that it is purely Bubbles, but she too is within the screenplay narrative. James extends the grotesquerie to include international points of cultural reference, beyond the scope of Bubbles' background, ensuring that the reader remains vulnerable to being interpellated into the narrative as reader.

The opening passages of *Black Sunlight* make Anglo-European culture and literary writing function like Conrad's Kurtz, where his narrator's body stands in for the 'body' of Africa as a feminine dark continent. Christian uses literary references with

---

[24] James, *Negrophobia*, 25-6.

a fierce irony, where 'all Europe had contributed to the making of Kurtz'[25] in *Heart of Darkness*, all globalized culture goes into the making of Christian's narrative, from Anglo-American to European. In a similar way, Miéville's *The Scar* subtly places New Crobuzon in an analogous position as transcendental signifier, compounding readerly identification with Bellis' prejudice even in the diverse environs of Armada. As a pirate utopia, Armada, a floating city on the sea, permanently moves between possibilities. And since it is composed of the flotsam of multiple cultures, it is redolent of postmodern theoretical writing concerned with hybridity, nomadism and slippage, inevitably calling to mind Deleuze and Guattari's *Anti-Oedipus* and *A Thousand Plateaus*. 'Salt, the mongrel sailor's tongue' becomes everybody's mother-tongue by dint of the fact that it, like the city, floats and shifts fluidly.[26] 'Salt' is a fittingly symbolic name for it. After all, it presents an image of language as something that can form crystals both large and small or solutions of varying dilutions, always the same thing, positive and negative components, yet always different depending on conditions.

The events of *The Scar* exist within a system of shifting plateaus of power and authority, based as it is, in terms of plot and textuality, on the interstices of possibilities. Direction itself on Armada can only be defined by the relatively fixed point of the largest ship in the flotilla, the *Grand Easterly*, an old New Crobuzoner ship whose name and physical description directly recall Isambard Kingdom Brunel's *Great Eastern*:

> Almost nine hundred feet of black iron. Five colossal funnels and six masts stripped of canvas more than two hundred feet high; and tethered way above them a huge, crippled dirigible. A vast paddle on each side of the ship, like industrial sculptures.[27]

[25] Joseph Conrad, *Heart of Darkness* (1899; London: Penguin, 2000), 83.
[26] Miéville, *The Scar*, 75.
[27] Ibid., 83.

This ship determines the direction of movement of Armada as well; it is the power base of the mysterious Lovers and their ally, the warrior-philosopher Uther Doul. Their quest (one of several which drive the plot) is initiated from this ship and it is significant that the monomania which drives the mutually scarred lovers, like Ahab with his maimed leg and single white scar, is housed in a ship redolent of Victorian overreaching. Yet, this ship is helpless without the others around it which make it part of Armada. It is powerful *only* as a symbol, an image. Again, then, perception is credited as that which creates cultural power and has the potential to be manipulated.

Similarly, Marechera's narrator has entered the position of Conrad's Kurtz as he has imbibed his Oxford education, so that he is not the subject of a European Imperial power writing-back to the Imperial centre, but rather writing while saturated with the contradictions of an apparent end-of-Imperialism and continued cultural and economic dominance. He represents Hardt and Negri's notion of the subject of Empire.

Christian, doubling Marechera, actively takes up the cultural fragments which postmodernity makes his, and finds new personal uses for them which play with the concept of authenticity in representation. Marechera's fictions are actively pirate and utopian, using the fragments of literature to mimetically track the transnational cultural exchanges of globalized culture as it impinges itself on individual subjectivity.

Both the 'Urban Parable' of *Negrophobia* and Miéville's *The Scar*, make markedly similar demands to those articulated in *Black Sunlight*. Each calls for urgent critical response to the deformations of contemporary consciousness from within the language which is also part of that deformation. The forms of cultural misapprehension these texts attack are part of a complex of gendered and sexualized relations of image and culture of the spectacular society. If, as Hardt and Negri argue, there is no space outside of Empire from which to launch an attack on it, then any resistance must come from, and acknowledge its own position within, the globalized spectacular society. Hardt and Negri identify the manipulation of language and image of the spectacular society with the management of identity politics which characterizes postmodernity.

Black Sunlight, *Negrophobia*, and *The Scar* make the manipulation of image and perception through words, particularly written words, central to their function as texts by exposing their own manipulation of the reader through the expectations created by formal conventions. At the conclusion of *The Scar*, the Armadans meet a deserter from their ship/city who claims to be an alternate-universe version of their deserter who has witnessed Armada reach the object of its quest and plunge with all inhabitants into the infinite depths of the Scar; the mode of representation has prepared the reader for the possibility of authentic representation from the fantastic but the text denies certainty in favour of interpretive possibility. In this way *The Scar* thematizes its own fantasy status by comparing genre with social convention – the Armadans accept the story and turn back from the brink. This realizes the grounds on which previous sub-plots within the novel have been problematized: perception and charismatic authority. The novel has a double conclusion based on textual uncertainty. The perceived possible destruction of Armada and Bellis' flawed perception and speculation about the future of her own narrative, both of which play upon readerly perception. Similarly, *Negrophobia* uses stereotype and caricature, presented as exaggerated images which are to be projected on a hypothetical screen, drawing clear attention to the relationship of stereotype/caricature to psychological projection. In this way, the text questions its own completeness and authenticity *as text* in much the same way as Marechera's Christian meeting his author in *Black Sunlight* or the double conclusion of *The Scar*.

Miéville shows us glimpses of many different societies in *The Scar*, telling us stories about them from different perspectives throughout the novel. A central contention of *The Scar* is that cultural hybridity can function to incorporate, differentiate and manage individuals within society, which means it is a form of control as well as of liberation:

'It's a misconception,' he said, 'to think that High Cromlech is all thanati. The quick are there too … We are a minority, it's true. And of those born every year many are farm-bred, kept in cages till they're of strength, when they can be snuffed and recast as zombies. Others are raised by the aristocracy until they come of age, and are slain and welcomed to dead society. But…'

His voice petered out, and he became introspective for a moment. 'But then there's Liveside. The ghetto. That's where the true quick live. My mother was prosperous. We lived at the better end.'

'There are jobs that only the living can do. Some are manual, too dangerous to risk giving to zombies – they're expensive to animate, but one can always breed more of the quick.' His voice was deadpan. 'And for those lucky enough, for the cream – the livemen and livewifes, the quick gentry – there are the taboo jobs that the thanati won't touch, at which the quick can make a decent living.'[28]

This speech indicates that all categories which can be understood as transgressive in one sense can also be understood in terms of their ability to incorporate, differentiate, and manage. The distinctions between living, dead and undead which might be presumed to represent an epistemological transgression of category, defying social power, are here posited as lived ways of reinforcing the class and race-based divides of social power – there are the 'Quick,' both 'farm-bred' and 'true-live,' the 'Thanati,' zombies and the 'ab-dead.'

Miéville's epigraph for *The Scar* reproduces the concluding lines of *Black Sunlight*, in a passage which unifies subjective and objective images in a disjunctively surrealist way returning the reader to the conflict between authentic and inauthentic representation:

---

[28] Miéville, *The Scar*, 334.

Yet the memory would not set into the setting sun, that green and frozen glance to the wide blue sea where broken hearts are wrecked out of their wounds. A blind sky bleached white the intellect of human bone, skinning the emotions from the fracture to reveal the grief underneath. And the mirror reveals me, a naked and vulnerable fact.[29]

These lines remake Christian from meaningful character into a function of the act of making meaning from abstract narrative, but they assert rather than diminish his significance, as such, to the reader. Coming at the beginning of a fantasy novel, which seems to present quest narrative conventions as a concrete, internally consistent world, such slippage between representation and subjectivity seems confusing, or deliberately obscurantist, but when re-read in context of the oblique counter-quest narrative of *The Scar*, Marechera's ambiguity becomes clear. Christian's cyclical journey, as a journey through attempts at representation, is echoed by that of Bellis Coldwine. The reader and Bellis only hear about the place that is the object of the most powerful quest on Armada, to the 'Scar' itself. It is a location where pure possibilities (quantum possibilities, alternate worlds, alternate lives and structures) all exist simultaneously. But it is a location that the reader never sees since the notion of infinite possibility defies the possibility of representation. When Bellis concludes the novel by finishing her epistle/journal, terming it a 'Possible Letter,' she is intimating something to the reader about text-as-text. That impossible means (the fantastic, the avant-garde) are perhaps the most effective means of grasping the real qualities of life under postmodernity where all meta-narratives appear to co-exist.[30]

Negrophobia raises the same important question of authenticity versus inauthenticity in representation and places it at

[29] Marechera, *Black Sunlight*, 117.
[30] Miéville, *The Scar*, 603-4.

the point of vulnerability to interpretative violence. Before the narrative begins the reader is presented with a disclaimer in the front matter which states: 'NEGROPHOBIA is a work of fiction, a product of the author's imagination … *Negrophobia* is a work of fiction. Every word is true.' The important point about this disclaimer is that it draws a distinction between imaginary text and actual text in terms of authentic experience: 'NEGROPHOBIA' refers to the hypothetical film, while *Negrophobia* refers to the text in hand. Here, the text in hand is the source of confrontational 'truth,' but as a text it is composed of the body of the hypothetical film text which is product of pure imagination and which claims that 'resemblance' to reality or real people is 'purely coincidental' (adding to the effect, James even makes the disclaimer resemble a verse poem).

Analogously, throughout *Black Sunlight* there are moments of deliberate semic slippage, between physical description of character, material description of the immediate environment and psychological description of their mind state as subject which precisely question the grounds of authenticity in representation. Marechera employs generic idioms of 'pulp' genre and the 'literary' to embody ideological positions towards the environment and subjective mood and ideological pressure as lived forces, aspects of the real which, he suggests, cannot be conveyed through social realism:

> Way up there, deep in the abyss. The way of the insider. Where the moon and the sixpence still twinkle over the violet Pacific nights. Where the sound and the fury still blows over the deep south. And golden notebooks tell of the tensions that travel through the white-hot wires from Cape Town to Dumfriesshire. But the Nazi ironclad churns closer. Its gun lashes out anew.[31]

Here, Marechera uses literary and cultural allusion as invocations which cause a certain disjuncture which we can character-

---

[31] Dambudzo Marechera, *The Black Insider*, ed. Flora Veit-Wild (Trenton, NJ: Africa World Press, 1992), 113.

ize as surrealist. The central image defies historical realism in favour of a trans-historical literary allusion. The abyss is arguably that of History itself, suggesting that Marechera sees a parallel between himself and Modernism. Indeed, the dream-like nature of this scene and its apocalyptic overtones link it with both Walter Benjamin's catastrophic vision of history given in his 'Theses on the Philosophy of History'[32] and the Joycean nightmare of history.[33] The churning ironclad is an abstract image, it suggests the European vessel shelling the jungle in Conrad's *Heart of Darkness* but rather than imagining such a thing as a description of the literal rendered absurdist, the anachronistic addition of 'Nazi' constructs it as a symbolic force of trans-historical European violence where the destructiveness of European modernity becomes globalized postmodernity.

The reader is presented with a radical uncertainty as to the authenticity of representation through a form of double-voicing similar to those of Marechera and Miéville where their texts employ the conventions of social realism and quest fantasy. *Black Sunlight*, *Negrophobia*, and *The Scar* all conclude by laying bare their own textuality and uncertainty as their most appropriate and authentic representational function: the naked and vulnerable fact becomes the text as an attempt to engage with postmodernity, imparted to the reader as a necessary ambiguity towards authenticity when attempting to grasp 'the real' in a globalized culture.

Hardt and Negri describe Empire as the totality of exchanges which define global culture; it is maintained and regulated everywhere and all at once by cultural regulation at personal, regional, national, and international levels, to which any resistance can only be formulated in terms of its ability to negate the networks of power which produce identity, truth, and politics in a globalized world through the management

---

[32] Walter Benjamin, 'Theses on the Philosophy of History' (1940), in *Illuminations: Essays and Reflections*, trans. Harry Zorn (London: Pimlico, 1999), 249.
[33] James Joyce, *Ulysses: The 1922 Text* (1922; Oxford: Oxford UP, 2008).

of difference. They observe that the management of difference constitutes a major aspect of any imperial strategy:

> More often than not, the Empire does not create division but rather recognizes existing or potential differences, celebrates them, and manages them within a general economy of command. The triple imperative of the Empire is incorporate, differentiate, manage.[34]

I have argued that the thematic echoes between Marechera, James and Miéville are as much a result of engaging in a struggle against the forms of representation which support postmodernity in globalized culture as they are a conscious or unconscious intertextuality. They are all seeking to expose the ways that cultural expression is incorporated, differentiated, and managed to reproduce the dominant ideology of globalization.

I suggest that we consider the fiction of Marechera in terms of its relationships with other radical texts as families of avant-gardism which do not need to be related to one another directly but are all engaging directly with the international cultural exchanges we call postmodernity at the totalizing level identified by Hardt and Negri. Writing such as Marechera's gives a sense of how to grasp, generate and reproduce a critical aesthetic position that is simultaneously undifferentiated (universalist, internationalist literature) and unassimilated (idiosyncratic, refusenik), and thereby unmanaged, in the midst of globalization. *Black Sunlight* is a revitalizing example and inspiration to those who seek to push the boundaries of representation beyond individuated concepts of culture towards the ideal of a literature of globalization and it is culturally significant to us all that its resonances can be felt in works as diverse as Darius James' *Negrophobia* and China Miéville's *The Scar*.

---

[34] Hardt and Negri, *Empire*, 201.

8 Classical Allusion in Marechera's Prose Works

MADHLOZI MOYO

This chapter addresses a key issue in the hermeneutics of the Marechera prose corpus, namely the author's use of allusions to the Greco-Roman experience: literature, mythology, culture, and so on. While some critics have dedicated a lot of space to attacking Marechera's use of classical allusion in his literature, others have defended Marechera on that same score. Obert Mlambo says that classical literature cannot be separated from the writings of Marechera. 'To separate the two,' he writes, 'is like throwing away the baby together with bath water.'[1] Marechera himself dedicates ample time in defense of his use of Greco-Roman scenery to adorn his works. This chapter attempts, within this narrow scope, to identify some of the most significant classical allusions in his prose, and thereby to understand better their contribution to the meaning of the texts. That is to say, I want to question the inheritance and explore the intertextual significance of classical allusion in Marechera's prose works. Of course, Marechera offers too many allusions to the ancient western world to consider offering an exhaustive account here. So, this present research introduces a bigger project to come, which will look at all classical allusions in Marechera's writing. In the meantime, I address the most recurrent classicisms in the prose corpus, and discuss those themes that strike me as the product of an African mind trained in the classics.

In a discussion held with a gathering of curious students, the narrator of *Black Sunlight*, who we might like to read as

---

[1] Obert Mlambo, 'Resurrecting the Teaching of Classics in Zimbabwe's Secondary Schools: The Imperative for a New Paradigm in Zimbabwe's Education Approach,' *Zimbabwe Journal of Educational Research* 23, no. 1 (2011), 55.

Marechera, says, 'I am astonished at the audience's ignorance. I did not expect such a low cultural level among you. Those who do not understand my work are simply illiterate. One must learn.'[2] It seems that Marechera is responding to a charge that has been leveled against him, here – namely that he is a difficult avant-garde artist. As Flora Veit-Wild suggests, this is precisely why Heinemann rejected *The Black Insider*. A reader's report on Marechera's manuscript concludes,

> It is very much overlaid with classical allusions which, frankly, do not seem to fit into the novel at all. More than that I do not think they are of interest to the general reader and this is what we as publishers have to bear in mind: that we have to publish books that people will enjoy reading and will not cost them too much in terms of time and effort![3]

Here, then, is the recurrent charge made against Marechera's apparently unseemly use of classical allusions and anecdotes. However, I share the same view as John Wylie. For me, these 'difficult' allusions only serve to render the complexity while at the same time anchoring Marechera's very original thoughts. Commenting on such allusions in *The Black Insider*, Wylie writes,

> There are, of course, too many of them … but they are not dragged in just for the effect. All the quotations are germane to Marechera's arguments though their use does, on occasion, make the book read like a clever dissertation for a PhD. What makes it remarkable is that the author, with so many brilliant minds supporting him and his ability to draw on them, can still find a wealth of original and perfectly phrased statements of his own to forward arguments and to throw light on his own ideas.[4]

Undoubtedly, Marechera is a classicizing author, and his use of the classical idiom suggests that he sees some kind of value

---

[2] Dambudzo Marechera, *Black Sunlight* (London: Heinemann, 1980), 110.

[3] Flora Veit-Wild, introduction to *The Black Insider*, by Dambudzo Marechera (Harare: Baobab Books, 1990), 12.

[4] Ibid., 17.

in the idea of classical humanism. Indeed, based on the sheer proliferation of classical thought in his writing, one may begin to think of Marechera as a universal humanist. 'The task of the universal humanist,' Daniela Volk says, 'is to search endlessly for common experiences of reality and ways of communicating the different expressions of those experiences. This task is in opposition to the postmodern claim that reality can be understood and represented only in particular and local forms.'[5] It is this fine line between universal commonality and local specificity that Marechera walks. In this context, George Kahari finally decides that Marechera's 'message is not only appealing to the moral sentiment of his own people, but the sentiment of all mankind – the universal man.'[6] Indeed, Marechera's writing seems to be intimately political in nature. After all, he is writing during a crucial time when Zimbabwe is engaged in nation building, which would suggest that he hopes in some way to sway the way in which people are thinking about the nationalist rhetoric that is circulating. In any case, this complex political situation leads the Marechera of *The Black Insider* to draw attention to the dialectic of the universal and the local through, typically, classical allusion. Invoking the voices of Heraclitus and Sophocles, Marechera writes, 'The old Greek Philosopher said "everything flows." And Sophocles could only mumble "These things are not of today or yesterday, but of all times, and no man knows when they appeared".'[7] At the very least, this demonstrates the subtle, unannounced, way in which Marechera turns to the thought of the ancient Mediterranean in order to explain the realities of his own times. For some, this is the key problematic in Marechera's eclectic style. After all, what does ancient Greece have to do with twentieth-century Zimbabwe?

---

[5] Daniela Volk, '"In Search of my True People:" Universal Humanism in Marechera's Writing,' in *Emerging Perspectives on Dambudzo Marechera*, eds. Flora Veit-Wild and Anthony Chennells (Trenton, NJ: Africa World Press, 1999), 300.

[6] George Kahari, *The Search for Identity and Ufuru* (Gweru: Mambo Press, 2009), 189.

[7] Dambudzo Marechera, *The Black Insider*, ed. Flora Veit-Wild (Harare: Baobab Books, 1990), 86.

For Marechera, thought transcends time and place. This is the kind of universalism in which Marechera is interested. But, it clearly stands at odds with the influential literary aesthetic promoted by Fay Chung and Emmanuel Ngara – that Zimbabwean or African literature should belong to the school of critical socialist realism, and it should abound in images generated from indigenous African experience, like African myths and folktales. That is to say, it should serve the nation-building effort. Such a discourse becomes extremely sour when the proponents of critical socialist realism attempt to tell writers what to write. Ngara's program for the production of 'acceptable' literature reads, 'First, telling the story truthfully and plainly, without "artificial" complications and adornments; second, presenting *typical characters*; and third, reproducing these characters under typical circumstances.'[8] However, very few writers want to be told what and how to write. And Marechera is notorious for being incompliant in nearly every aspect of his life! So it is that he blends traditional Shona imagery with that of the classics – the 'manfish' of the 'The Writer's Grain' meets Ariadne of *Mindblast*; the Second Chimurenga is understood by allusion to the Trojan War.[9]

Ultimately, this collision of the African and the European, the old and the new, the rural and the metropolitan complicates the matter of African authenticity as outlined by Maurice Vambe. He explains,

> In their struggles to maintain a sense of cultural identity and autonomy, Africans adopted from their past forms of oral literature such as song, dance, and folktales and forged new ones... This incorporated orality as a stylistic strategy to give a stamp of 'African' authenticity to their works of art.[10]

[8] Emmanuel Ngara, *Art and Ideology in the African Novel: A Study of the Influence of Marxism on African Writing* (London: Heinemann, 1985), 14.

[9] For an excellent discussion of Marechera's use of traditional Shona imagery in his writing see Grant Lilford, 'Traces of Tradition: The Probability of the Marecheran Manfish,' in *Emerging Perspectives on Dambudzo Marechera*, 283-98.

[10] Maurice Taonezvi Vambe, *African Oral Story-telling Tradition and the Zimbabwean*

Marechera's willingness to blend such 'authentic' markers of African literature with images drawn from classical European tradition in order to present a new way of seeing and thinking about contemporary Zimbabwe, gave rise to some harsh criticism of his writing. Drew Shaw cites Musaemura Zimunya, Mbulelo Mzamane, and Juliet Okonkwo as being among those who position themselves in opposition to Marechera's non-conformism to African literary tradition and the socialist realist aesthetic privileged in post-colonial Zimbabwe. Ranga Zinyemba says, 'If Nyamfukudza is a descendant of the British and European Decadence, Marechera is his cousin, for indeed, as in the case of Conrad's Kurtz, all Europe contributed to the making of Marechera.'[11] Marechera is quite combative about what he sees as reductive measures to try and situate him into a particular literary canon or agenda. He writes, 'If you are a writer for a specific nation or a specific race, then fuck you.'[12] His refusal to conform to the so-called African way of writing has earned him epithets that range from 'the verbal gimmick Marechera' to 'the literary sellout Marechera.' Nevertheless, Marechera clearly refuses to be confined or defined in line with the rhetoric of the newly independent African state. His work is influenced by a lot of authors from around the world, but it is certainly from the Western literary tradition that he draws most frequently. Indeed, As Kahari states, 'An unignorable aspect of Marechera's writing is the influence of his Western education and his exposure to a tremendous amount of its literature.'[13] The major reason for this, according to Kahari, is the fact that Marechera did not experience the kind of rural upbringing which is associated with other Zimbabwean writers such as Stanlake Samkange, Wilson Katiyo, and Charles Mungoshi.

(contd) *Novel in English* (Pretoria: UNISA Press, 2004), 2.

[11] Ranga Zinyemba, 'Zimbabwe's "Lost" Novelists in Search of Direction,' *Moto* 15, no. 7 (August 1983), 10.

[12] Flora Veit-Wild, *Dambudzo Marechera: A Source Book on his Life and Work* (London: Hans Zell, 1992), 121.

[13] Kahari, *The Search for Identity and Ufuru*, 191.

It is this, Kahari suggests, that partly explains Marechera's implacable refusal to appeal to those values of the past, or to romanticize its traditions.

It is in this context that Marechera turns towards Western literary antiquity in his writing. James Tatum points out that,

> Antiquity offered specific models for imitation and adaptation by later writers: scandalous tales from Apuleius's *Golden Ass* reworked and sprinkled over the *Decameron*, to equally scandalous effect; Lucian's *True History* begetting *Gulliver's Travels*, Heliodorus's *Ethiopian Story*, Cervantes.[14]

To this list we should add Marechera. Technically, Marechera's prose works are *satura*. In the circles of ancient literary criticism, the term *satura* entails the mingling of prose, poetry, literary parody, and philosophy within a single work. *Satura* first assumed its literary form in the hands Mennipus of Gadara, Syria in the third century BC – hence the term 'Mennipean satire.' *Satura* is a term that properly refers to a sacrificial meal for the gods of ancient Greece and Rome, consisting of a variety of fruits and analogized in literature as a mixing of prose, poetry, and philosophy, the like of which is easy to find in Marechera's writing – 'Tomorrow homeless who today are reckless,' we are told in *The Black Insider*.[15] However, it is because of this marriage of genres that Marechera's publishers had problems classifying his books as novels, referring to them simply as 'unstructured.' For example, James Currey read *The Black Insider* and *A Bowl for Shadows* and, as Veit-Wild writes, 'While he recognized the manuscripts as "brilliant" and "full of excellence," he wanted them to be further developed and shaped into proper novel form, "particularly in terms of plot and characterisation".'[16] Like the ancient novel, Marechera's prose is a potpourri of

---

[14] James Tatum ed., *The Search for the Ancient Novel* (Baltimore: John Hopkins UP, 1994), 2.

[15] Marechera, *The Black Insider*, 41.

[16] Veit-Wild, introduction to *The Black Insider*, 7.

literary types. Indeed, Marechera's novels seem to repeat the dynamic that Daniel Selden sees in Petronius' *The Satyricon*. He writes, Petronius

> presents the reader with a dazzling display of generic composition: ecphrasis, satire, a Milesian tale, diatribe, and epyllion all follow in rapid succession, juxtaposing vulgar with elite, poetry with prose, anecdote with declamation. The separate pieces are connected by the common theme of decadence, physical as well as moral, which each develops from its own generically specific point of view.[17]

The best examples of this fluidity of expression in Marechera's oeuvre are *The Black Insider*, *Mindblast* and, in its present edited form, *Scrapiron Blues*. For example, within the first twenty pages of *The Black Insider* the narrative has cycled through prose, verse – in an emulation of Shelley's play *Prometheus Unbound* (1820) – and drama. The flow of the narrative and themes remains uninterrupted even with this shift from one genre to the next. Shelley's poem, for example, is a recitation that compliments an initial attack on the political scenario of the coalition government that was formed between Bishop Abel Muzorewa and Ian Smith. The prose reads, 'It is not enough to be in power but to be power itself and there is no such thing except in the minds of people with religious notions.' Six lines further down comes the poetry of Shelley's play, 'Go, borne over the cities of mankind/ On whirlwind-footed courses: once again.'[18] After this we shift back to prose, and then quickly fall into a drama:

Marota: He has made a joke of us.
Bishop: I'll laugh while it lasts.[19]

The significance of the dramatic set piece here, is that it explores the politics of the transitional administration of Zimbabwe-Rhodesia era. So it is that the names of the characters have direct historical equivalents – Smith represents Ian

---

[17] Daniel Selden, 'Genre of Genre,' in *The Search for the Ancient Novel*, 41.
[18] Marechera, *The Black Insider*, 37.
[19] Ibid., 38.

Smith; the Bishop, Abel Muzorewa, and so on. However, despite the shifts in genre, the reader is always aware of the major preoccupation of the novel, which is the burlesque of the coalition government and the necessity of total regime change. So, far from *The Black Insider* being an unstructured narrative, it is, in fact, 'hyper-structured.' What this means, as Viet-Wild recognizes of *The Black Insider*, is that

> What might seem unstructured at first sight turns out to have a strong inner coherence if the reader is prepared to follow the writer along paths of thought which, though intricate, are an intrinsic part of his work.[20]

Black Sunlight and *Mindblast* repeat this mélange of literary forms in order to chart a particular idea that is not, indeed, cannot, be limited to one specific form of expression. So, it is important to reiterate that Marechera's drawing together of genres is no mere copy and paste exercise. Rather, Marechera encourages this radical eclecticism of literary forms. And he does so in order to enliven, perhaps reinvigorate, the reading experience. Through this kind of writerly strategy, the reader is cast into a very active position. Marechera, it seems, is desperate for his reader to think about what he or she is reading, to consider the relationships between the forms that Marechera employs and the ideas that he interrogates.

It is in this sense that the treatment of political and philosophical concerns in *The House of Hunger*, *Black Sunlight*, and *Mindblast* casts a strong association with the *satura* tradition. For example, in *Mindblast*, Grimknife Junior says to his friend, 'You know, there is a guy in that hospital who thinks he is Socrates,' to which Buddy responds, 'I know the feeling, I once believed I was Catulus.'[21] It is a passage that recalls Aristophanes' *The Clouds*, since it too is a critique of intellectual fashions.

---

[20] Veit-Wild, introduction to *The Black Insider*, 13.
[21] Dambudzo Marechera, *Mindblast, or, The Definitive Buddy* (Harare: College Press, 1984), 57.

However, just this minor aside in the narrative encourages one to consider the connection between the intellectually broken figure of Socrates in *Mindblast* and the comic figure presented by Apuleius in *The Golden Ass*. Similarly, the prominence of the Cicero character in *The Black Insider* assures the reader that there is ample philosophizing going on:

> Cicero, my neighbor who is always shouting obscenities about the 'warmongering' bastards, actually wears a toga and bowler hat … He, in fact, studied at RADA and did some minor roles in *The Satyricon* and in the *Golden Ass* for an obscure provincial company in the backyard of Scotland… He is in his late forties, grey and balding, and has the most expensive looking tic on the left half of his clean shaven face. There is in his right eye a dusky Latin which is perpetually piercing the marrow of whomever he is talking to.[22]

Marechera's Cicero is of course modeled on the Roman politician, orator, and philosopher Marcus Tullius Cicero. He repeats the dress of his more noted namesake with the curious addition of the bowler hat, which perhaps symbolizes the cultural hybridism of Marechera's work. In any case, it highlights the fact that Marechera thought it quite ridiculous to unthinkingly borrow from different traditions. Marechera's Cicero is a ridiculous figure, someone to be lampooned. But, importantly, he is not to be lampooned because he draws from different traditions – the toga, the bowler hat, and so on – but because he is unable to synthesize these different traditions. It is this inability, then, that is the worthy site of Marechera's biting wit.

However, this gentle comic tone gives way to a more acerbic kind of satire in other areas of Marechera's prose work. Indeed, his objects of satire are wide ranging, including the politically powerful – politicians like Ian Smith and Bishop Muzorewa, in *The Black Insider*, Fidel Castro and Richard Nixon in *Scrapiron Blues*, and so on – and the everyday man. Often Marechera

---

[22] Marechera, *The Black Insider*, 45.

re-establishes the genetic link between this kind of satire and the 'raunchy' tone of the satyr play. So, taking his lead from Apuleius, who writes of cheating wives, bestiality, and other base activities in *The Golden Ass*, and Petronius, whose *The Satyricon* revolves around the often sexual misadventures of the anti-hero, Encolpius, Marechera pens Fred, who narrates the bawdy tales of *Scrapiron Blues*. In fact, it is difficult to resist the temptation to think of the tales presented in *Scrapiron Blues* as anything other than a twentieth century rewriting of Apuleius' stories. For example, in the 'Tale of the Tub,' Apuleius makes a critique on cheating wives which is almost identical to the first short story in *Scrapiron Blues*, 'Smith in Dead Skin.' In both stories, both wives' husbands accidentally come home because there is no work to do, and they stumble on their wives having extramarital sex. And in both cases the cheating wives get their lovers out of the way by duping their husbands to actually assist in the evacuation of the lovers. Surprisingly, though, it is Apuleius who takes the scenario further, because the legitimate husband is compelled to get into an overturned bath tub, on top of which his wife and her lover proceed to have more sex.

Marechera also uses these texts, particularly *The Satyricon*, to allude to dictatorship, censorship, and the persecution of authors by governments. Importantly, Petronius fell out of favor with the Roman emperor Nero and was ordered to commit suicide, which he consummated by opening up the veins on his wrists. For Marechera, the persecution and incarceration of authors such as Mongo Beti, Ngugi wa Thiong'o, and Wole Soyinka by their respective governments not only seems to be an almost incomprehensible repetition of State censorship but also the repetition of the barbarism of the State. Thousands of years may separate the acts of government, but Marechera shows that it is the same vindictiveness and desire for power that remains at the core of such political maneuvers. In *The Black Insider*, he writes,

Mongo Beti's story of the old man and the medal had clearly come home to roost. Petronius would feel quite at home there – until of course his own veins are opened. Our search for freedom has not included the most elementary humanitarian justice.[23]

So, in this passage Marechera uses Petronius' tragedy to draw parallels with the silencing of African authors by political authorities in the newly independent African state. Of course, it is something that also draws parallels to Marechera's own brush with the CIO. In any case, the use of *The Satyricon*, here, though it might mean nothing to an average Zimbabwean who has not read the surviving fragments of Petronius' text, is very apt in demonstrating Marechera's concern for freedom of speech.

His references to Caligula in *The Black Insider* and elsewhere invokes perhaps a more obvious image. Caligula, the by-name for cruel and inept leaders, was fond of extravagant shows during the early times of his emperorship, though his dive into insanity is perhaps the way in which most like to characterize him. Like the black chief in the opening pages of *Black Sunlight* who sits on a throne of skulls and orders his guards to hang the narrator head-down in a chicken coup,[24] Caligula has similar wild flourishes. He once proclaimed himself a divinity; reportedly committed incest with his sisters Drusilla, Agrippina, and Julia Livia; and derailed an expedition to attack Britain by ordering the soldiers to gather sea-shells. It is, then, as though Marechera could not find a better image for the typically inept, 'mad' African politician than this tyrant from European history.

It seems certain that Marechera's fondness for the classics is a result of his wide reading at both the University of Rhodesia and Oxford. As such, it seems almost inevitable that he should draw from the classical world in order to understand better the texture of contemporary Zimbabwe. The question, though, is who benefits from this intersection of European and African

---

[23] Ibid., 85.
[24] Marechera, *Black Sunlight*, 3.

thought? In responding to this question, George Kahari posits that *Black Sunlight*, at least, is a novel that is written for a Western readership – it is a novel that tries to reveal the tortured soul of an African nation and the role that Western powers played in damaging it. Talking of Marechera, he writes, 'because Westernization influenced him, it follows that he wishes his work to be looked at in a similar light and once again, feed the irony that infiltrates the novel.'[25] This sentiment, though, is something with which I find difficult to agree. Indeed, I think it is particularly problematic to think that Marechera 'aimed' his writing at any specific group of people. Undoubtedly, Marechera would vigorously defend himself against this charge. Perhaps, then, the best way to look at the matter is to think of Marechera as simply writing in order to present his combative ideas about the relationship between State and Society, Society and the People. It is in this context that I would like my chapter to draw to a close by quoting from Daniela Volk and Drew Shaw, both of whom direct the following questions to the critics who attack Marechera's use of classical imagery. Volk says,

> The world has produced many people like Marechera who dare to celebrate difference and attempt to communicate across difference. A society which has no place for someone like him is a long way from being free and almost certainly is a long way from regarding its members as possessing equal rights.[26]

Similarly, Drew Shaw asks of the proponents of the socialist realist aesthetic, 'Who are they to judge what "African tradition" or "Zimbabwean authenticity" is?'[27] Marechera's insistence on using allusions from classical Western literature, with such fierce conceptual force, amounts to a statement that there is no *a priori* limit that can be placed on what can or cannot be used or said!

[25] Kahari, *The Search for Identity and Ufuru*, 196.
[26] Volk, 'In Search of my True People,' 311.
[27] Drew Shaw, 'Transgressing Traditional Narrative Form,' in *Emerging Perspectives on Dambudzo Marechera*, 8.

9

Revisiting
'The Servants' Ball'

MEMORY CHIRERE

The concerns of this chapter are threefold. First, it highlights the fact that Dambudzo Marechera's play 'The Servants' Ball'[1] is the only known artistic work in Marechera's oeuvre written in his mother tongue, Shona. Second, it shows how Marechera's play is situated in the context of the newly independent Zimbabwe of the early 1980s. And, finally, this chapter explores how the 'discovery' of Marechera's only Shona work resurrects the 'ghost' of the debate over the 'appropriate' language of African literature.

For many Zimbabweans, it is not necessary to have read *The House of Hunger* or *Mindblast* to know Dambudzo Marechera. He is public property. For the teenage reader, the name Dambudzo Marechera is synonymous with rebelliousness. For the many writers across Zimbabwe, the name evokes razor sharp brilliance. There is the mental image of the stubborn, dreadlocked man furiously writing, and writing, and writing. The youngsters often wish that they are him – that they have his vision, language and charisma. However, when one has worshipped Marechera like this, one begins to wonder if he ever wrote in his mother tongue. Such absence in his literary production is made glaring by the fact that some of Marechera's contemporaries and friends, like Charles Mungoshi, Musaemura Zimunya and Chenjerai Hove, have actually written convincingly in both English and Shona and, moreover, won prizes in both languages.

In an interview with Flora Veit-Wild, Chenjerai Hove states

[1] Dambudzo Marechera, 'The Servants' Ball,' in *Scrapiron Blues* (Harare: Baobab Books, 1994), 61-72 in Shona; 73-84 in English. Unless indicated otherwise, further page references will be given in the main text from the English version of the play.

that for him the choice of which language to use in a particular story or poem is finally determined by the experience being captured in the story or poem. He explains, 'The experience tells me that this would be captured in Shona and sometimes the experience comes in English, and if I wrote it in Shona, it wouldn't be the same.'[2] Perhaps this is why, at least once, Marechera sat down and wrote in Shona. Of course, he wrote 'The Servants' Ball,' which was published posthumously in *Scrapiron Blues*. The play itself is the sequel to 'The Toilet,' which was published in *Mindblast*,[3] but as Veit-Wild makes clear in her introduction to *Scrapiron Blues*, the publisher chose to omit it.[4] Recognizing the value of Marechera's only existent work in Shona, Veit-Wild takes care to include both the original Shona version and translated English version of the play in *Scrapiron Blues*. Indeed, the English version, translated so ably by Leonard Maveneka and Richard Mhonyera, follows directly after the Shona version.

It is not difficult to place the play. Other than being in Shona, 'The Servants' Ball' is in the mode of other *Mindblast* plays, those such as 'The Toilet,' 'The Coup,' 'The Gap,' and several others which satirize the new African elite and their local and international white racist and corrupt associates for not showing responsibility in their exercise of power and business. These Marechera plays connect the social rot in Zimbabwe with international capital and the white Rhodesian culture of plunder and segregation. Structurally, as Owen Seda rightly observes, these plays are relatively short 'one act' plays, which produce the effect of a 'snapshot' of life. He writes that the play 'is essentially a snapshot ... where the reader is immediately plunged into an abrupt climax even as the play opens.'[5] Written

[2] Flora Veit-Wild, *Patterns of Poetry in Zimbabwe* (Gweru: Mambo Press, 1988), 39.
[3] Dambudzo Marechera, *Mindblast, or, The Definitive Buddy* (Harare: College Press, 1984).
[4] Flora Veit-Wild, introduction to *Scrapiron Blues*, by Dambudzo Marechera (Harare: Baobab Books, 1994), xii.
[5] Owen Seda, 'The Fourth Dimension: Dambudzo Marechera as a Dramatist – An

in scintillating Chiungwe, the dialect dominant in Marechera's Rusape district in Zimbabwe's Eastern province, 'The Servants' Ball' is an attack on the corruption of the newly independent Zimbabwe society. Indeed, it captures the anger and apprehension of the people following the Willowgate scandal,[6] which netted some very prominent politicians who had been involved in underhand business deals during the 1980s.

The setting for 'The Servants' Ball' is the servants' quarters at a white employer's residence in Harare. Here a number of garden boys, nannies, cooks, and other colleagues are drinking, chattily reflecting on their lives, political independence, and the impending Christmas season. The satirical atmosphere of the play is facilitated by the fact that the drama takes place at a beer drink whose register in Shona traditions allows people to say things aloud that they would not normally say. That is to say, the beer place in the Shona tradition allows suspension of formal language when addressing others. The characters of the play, therefore, are free and uninhibited in their use of language and expression of their views. Marechera uses this technique as a convenient, indeed clever, facility to take off the leash of inhibition in matters of coarse language and subject matter. Later on, when sober, the attendees of such beer parties can always dismiss unpalatable or confrontational pronouncements as 'Zvepahwahwa' – that is to say, nonsensical issues from a beer party that need to be set aside from further, perhaps serious, consideration. As a result, one can see regular use of crude statements in Marechera's play, such as Mberi's assertion that, 'You young people of today are just a load of shit thrown in

(contd) Analysis of Two Plays,' in *Zimbabwean Transitions: Essays on Zimbabwean Literature in English, Ndebele and Shona*, ed. Mbongeni Z. Malaba and Geoffrey V. Davis (Amsterdam: Rodopi, 2007), 152.

6   The 'Willowgate scandal' concerned the allocation of motor vehicles to government officials, who then sold the vehicles onwards for a large profit. Geof Nyarota, editor of the *Chronicle* newspaper, outlines the unravelling of the scandal in his letter to the editor of Zimbabwe's *The Standard* newspaper. See Geof Nyarota, 'Willowgate Revisited Two Decades Later,' *The Standard*, April 16, 2006, accessed May 5, 2011, http://www.thestandard.co.zw/?view=article&id=15274.

the way of us older people' (75). Thomas, the cook-houseboy, responds to this provocation in an equally coarse fashion, 'You are really talking through your arse, old lady' (75).

This sense of the realistic is consolidated by the banter, chants, songs, and philosophies of the characters, which are characteristic of Zimbabwe in the 1980s. For instance, the anti-Muzorewa sentiments of the times are evident in Bonzo's statement, 'Who is mumbling things I can't hear? Because if I hear the sell-out (*dzakutsaku*) who is talking that rubbish I shall fix him' (75). In the context of the Zimbabwean liberation struggle discourse, which of course continued after the war with Ian Smith's forces had been won, the politician and clergyman Abel Muzorewa was, and continues to be, viewed as a 'sell-out' because he engaged in what was viewed as a compromising pact with the racist forces of Rhodesia. Muzorewa, Ndabaningi Sithole and the other non-exiled leaders inside Rhodesia, signed a conciliatory agreement with Ian Smith that paved the way for an interim government. However, this government was not recognized by the two most heavily armed and powerful liberation movements that operated out of Zimbabwe,[7] and so the war for total control continued until the elections of February, 1980. Nevertheless, the interim 'puppet government,' as it was called in nationalist circles, continued to send out military forces to attack guerilla posts in neighboring Zambia and Mozambique, and to maintain the privileged position of the white minority population.[8] It is for this reason that Bonzo's words above are a serious accusation in the newly independent Zimbabwe. Indeed, given the association, it was considered unsafe to be labeled a *dzakutsaku* (a Muzorewa foot soldier) in public.

Another powerful link with this formative era of Zimbabwe

[7] I refer to Robert Mugabe's Zimbabwe African National Union (ZANU) and Joshua Nkomo's Zimbabwe African People's Union (ZAPU).

[8] Joseph Mtisi, Munyaradzi Nyakudya, and Teresa Barnes, 'War in Rhodesia, 1965-1980,' in *Becoming Zimbabwe*, ed. Brian Raftopolous and Alois Mlambo (Weaver Press: Harare, 2009), 141-166.

comes from the mouth of the house girl, Sarah. At one point in the play she stands up and drunkenly sings a song that satirizes the existence of the so called 'minimum wage' in Zimbabwe. Also exposing the mundane and demeaning nature of housekeeping, she sings:

I have washed up the dishes
The white man has gone away
I have swept the house
The missis is drunk

Chorus:
Give me my minimum wage
I have no food at home
Give me my minimum wage
The house is clean and things have changed.
Give me my minimum wage
I say give me my minimum wage
Are you deaf, I say
Give me my minimum wage (75)

Read properly, the song can only be seen as a serious political protest. When Marechera was penning these lines the Ministry of Labour had stipulated that the minimum wage would curtail the abuse and underpayment of domestic servants. Before independence in 1980, white managers seemed to rule black workers through a mixture of racism and paternalism. At independence, while hostilities between black workers and their white employers continued, structures were immediately established to enable union representatives to negotiate better pay and working conditions. In light of the fact that many white business owners and managers refused to conform to the new labor regime,[9] the new government propagated a whole range of economic policies – two of the most important of which were

---

[9] Mark Shadur, 'Labour Relations in Zimbabwean Parastatal,' *Zambezia* 18, no. 1 (1991), 25-34.

the 'minimum wage' and the increased difficulty employers faced in legally relieving an employee of their position. The minimum wage Act of 1980 established a minimum wage of Z$85 (US$133) per month for industrial workers and Z$30 (US$47) per month for agricultural and domestic workers.[10] It is in this context that Sarah lampoons her employers, the kind of employers who would hold on to her pay even though it is very clear that it is worth very little.

Sarah goes on with her blistering song and her drink-mates sing along, but these revelers also mention the tendency of the new black employers to withhold pay from workers. Bonzo explains, 'What I don't like are the black chefs. They make you work like an ox in the field.' Granny Beri continues, 'You have to be careful with them. You may not be paid for three months in a row' (77-8). Exposing a terrible irony, Marechera shows that the new black elite have simply joined the fray, refusing to pay house workers in just the same way that white employers did before them. Yet, the white employer Drake, whose residence is being used for this gathering of friends and fellow workers, is liked by his servant Thomas. Certainly, some of this admiration is due to the fact that Drake pays Thomas Z$90 per month, which is far in advance of the $Z30 minimum wage; but mostly, this is due to the fact that the boundaries of the traditional master/servant relationship are not entirely respected by either Drake or Thomas. So, 'Comrade Drake' buys beer for Thomas' gatherings and gives him free food. The result, it seems, is a happier house.

Interestingly, Marechera also organizes a silent competition in this play between Bonzo, the mbira player, and Majazi, the guitar player. Bonzo and Majazi are subtly juxtaposed in order to portray the contest between traditional African ways (the mbira) and the 'new' western ways (the guitar) in contemporary

---

[10] 'Zimbabwe – Working Conditions,' Encyclopedia of the Nations, accessed May 5, 2011, http://www.nationsencyclopedia.com/economies/Africa/Zimbabwe-WORK ING-CONDITIONS.html.

Zimbabwean society. So it is that both artists improvise tunes that are relevant to the contemporary condition of Zimbabwe. Bonzo sings of the circularity of history and colonialism thus, 'Hii-iiye-iiye friends / The white men have died, we have taken the land / Hii-iiye-iiye the land has gone / Let's go to war' (74). It is the precursor to Bonzo's pronouncement that there is no future for Zimbabwe. The guitar player, Majazi responds:

> But you, old man, can you recall that before Independence you were getting paid only four dollars per month? But you are now being paid fifty dollars a month. And you are not even married. Your white employers are giving you free accommodation and food. You can afford to drink kachasu, so why are you talking about having no future? (75)

Here, then, is the voice of the modernizer in Zimbabwe. The one who sees the economic progress being made by ordinary workers in the newly independent Zimbabwe.

Another illuminating moment is when Thomas rushes into the main house in order to receive beer from his employer, Drake. When he returns he declares in English that all this free beer is a benefit of 'neo-colonialism.' His friends do not take lightly the use of an English word that they cannot quite understand. Indeed, they miss out on the fact that 'neo-colonialism' refers to a phenomenon that is continuing to affect their country. Amid this general sense of confusion, one question presents itself – if Thomas is with an all-Shona audience, why does he choose to speak in English at all? The mbira player, Bonzo, actually chastises Thomas, 'Talk in Shona if you are with Shona speakers. Talk in English if you are with English speakers' (80). Ignoring the fact that the term does not find an easy translation in Shona, Bonzo suspects this is simply an example of Thomas 'showing off' to the gathering of friends.

It is an accusation that has been leveled at Marechera, the celebrated writer who rarely expressed himself in Shona even though this play shows that he had the ability to do so. His fractured, discontinuous, confrontational, and experimental writing style, for some, looks much like an educated person demonstrating their learning at the cost of rigorous social commentary.[11] This characterization of Marechera means that to this day in Zimbabwe few prominent literary scholars, playwrights, or directors are aware that Marechera wrote in Shona. Unsurprisingly, then, 'The Servants' Ball' is the least cited and staged of all of Marechera's plays.

In matters of plot, 'The Servants' Ball' is stagnant. Indeed, it seems that one must first be conversant in the socio-political environment of 1980s Zimbabwe in order to fully appreciate the play. The only kind of development in the play is the realization that Raven, a black girl, is to marry Dick, a white boy. In itself, this is an important pointer to the spirit of reconciliation that swept across the newly independent Zimbabwe. But this stagnation of plot means that the focus of the play rests squarely on the dialogue of the characters. In true Marechera style, these dialogues descend into an awkward relationship with meaning, and therefore capture the spirit of what Martin Esslin termed 'the theatre of the absurd.'[12] Consider for example Raven's and Dick's entrance to the party:

> Alfie: I am merely fooling. Psychiatric greetings, not unlike the Rorschach Test.
> Dick: The pedagogue. What next?
> Raven: Sherlock Holmes.
> Dick: The architect of the Zimbabwe Ruins.
> Thomas: Vhigoroni.
> Dick: Goncharov's 'A Hero of Our Time.' (82)

Just what is being played out in this 'little game' is almost incomprehensible. Although such passages add to the interpretive

---

[11] See for example Juliet Okonkwo, 'A Review of *The House of Hunger*,' *Okike: An African Journal of New Writing* (June 1981), 87-91; and, Musaemura Zimunya, *Those Years of Drought and Hunger: The Birth of Black Zimbabwean Literature in English* (Gweru: Mambo Press, 1982).

[12] Martin Esslin, *The Theatre of the Absurd* (London: Eyre and Spottiswoode, 1962).

space of the play, I think it is fair to say that 'The Servants' Ball' has its limitations if one were to imagine it on stage. Most notably, it can only be fully appreciated by an audience with good command of both Shona and English because the characters sometimes go for long stretches speaking in English. Perhaps an even greater problem would be how to accurately render the vulgarity of the play, especially some of the more base language used by some of the characters. Whilst these could be easily said in English, in Shona these words and phrases deeply offend.

Perhaps it was these kinds of questions that made it difficult for Marechera to write in Shona. Nonetheless, in an 'interview' in which Marechera interviews himself, he declares his antagonistic relationship with the language. After asking himself whether he had ever thought of writing in Shona, Marechera answers:

> It never occurred to me. Shona was part of the ghetto daemon I was trying to escape. Shona had been placed within the context of a degraded, mindwrenching experience from which apparently the only escape was into the English language and education ... I took to the English language as a duck takes to water.[13]

However, a year earlier, it appears Marechera had already managed to position himself in opposition to Shona. Flora Veit-Wild remembers him saying at a gathering:

> In Zimbabwe... we have these two great indigenous languages, ChiShona and SiNdebele... Who wants us to keep writing these ShitShona and ShitNdebele languages, this missionary chicken-shit? Who else but the imperialists?[14]

Marechera could have been putting forward the argument that

---

[13] Flora Veit-Wild and Ernst Schade, *Dambudzo Marechera, 1952-1987* (Harare: Baobab Books, 1988), 6-8.
[14] Flora Veit-Wild, *Dambudzo Marechera: A Source Book on His Life and Work* (London: Hans Zell, 2004), 307.

the kind of Shona and Ndebele narratives churned out from the 1950s to 1980 were heavily manipulated by the establishment through the Southern Rhodesian Literature Bureau. Emmanuel Chiwome's study on this matter reveals that the Bureau was created as part of the Ministry of Information. One of its major objectives was to direct the novel along 'the path of least ideological resistance to the Rhodesian government.'[15] Its founding director, a Mr Krog, set out to search for subversive material in every manuscript before it was published. This was counter-productive to the development of the novel in Shona and Ndebele rendering it generally 'silent on contemporary socio-political crises'[16] and having characters who are 'neutral on colonial economic policies.'[17]

As a result of these influences, Chiwome shows how the Shona novel is torn between protesting against colonialism and, ironically, persuading the reader that colonialism delivered the black folk into modernity – or, put another, a higher plane of existence. The new urban setting is portrayed as destroying the Shona people's well being, their harmony and decency. Patrick Chakaipa's *Garandichauya* (1963) for example, operates in the same way. In this novel, the rise of the urban center is the rise of wildness and immorality. However, the veiled suggestion that black people should remain in the Tribal Trust Lands if they are going to make real sense of their lives, is rather startling.

If one considers Marechera's earlier utterances against the Shona language, the sudden realization that Marechera actually wrote a play in Shona, brings to the fore the decades old debate on the 'appropriate' language of African literature. It was formalized in Obiajunwa Wali's early essay 'The Dead End of African Literature?' Here he argues that 'the whole uncritical acceptance of English as the inevitable medium for educated African writing, is misdirected, and has no chance of advancing

---

[15] Emmanuel Chiwome, *A Social History of the Shona Novel* (Kadoma: Juta, 1996), 35.
[16] Ibid., 38.
[17] Ibid., 38.

African literature and culture.'[18] Among other things, Wali declares that literatures written in European languages cannot pass as African literature and so 'true' African literature may actually disappear from the face of the earth.

From there on, contributors to this debate have either sided with Wali or opposed him. So, the Ngugi wa Thiong'o of *Decolonising the Mind* clearly aligns himself with Wali. Ngugi categorically states that 'literature written by Africans in European languages' can only be thought of as 'Afro-European literature'[19] and notes that his own return to Gikuyu in his fictional writing is a quest for relevance. Wali's and Ngugi's position, then, seems to lend itself to the aggressively exclusivist project presented by Chinweizu and others in *Towards the Decolonization of African Literature*.[20] In this influential book, Chinweizu tries to outline the shape of a truly African literature. In doing so, he not only cautions against writing in English but also the attempt to turn towards any aspect of the European literary tradition. As such, writers like Wole Soyinka and Christopher Okigbo are singled out for their use of intentionally playful syntax and employment of private images. Such (European) literary maneuvers see Chinweizu label these celebrated writers as obscurantists, who therefore have only a minor role to play in the canon of 'African Literature.'

Speaking against this reading of African literature is the voice of Chinua Achebe. Achebe spells out in *Morning Yet on Creation Day* that 'for me there is no other choice. I have been given a language and I intend to use it.'[21] Achebe does not set out to write using Standard English but to make his English carry the unique Ibo imagination and sensibility – something he

---

[18] Obiajunwa Wali, 'The Dead End of African Literature?' *Transition* 10 (September 1963), 14.

[19] Ngugi wa Thiong'o, *Decolonising the Mind: The Politics of Language in African Literature* (Harare: Zimbabwe Publishing House; London: James Currey, 1981), 26-7.

[20] Chinweizu, Onwuchekwa Jemie, and Ihechukwu Madubuike, *Towards the Decolonization of African Literature* (London: Taylor & Francis, 1985).

[21] Chinua Achebe, *Morning Yet on Creation Day* (London: Heinemann, 1975), 62.

demonstrates in perhaps the most widely-read African novel of all-time, *Things Fall Apart*. He goes on to say, 'The price a world language (English) must be prepared to pay is submission to many different kinds of use.'[22]

Peter Vakunta also takes Achebe's side. He argues that African writers must be responsible for promoting the image of Africa that they render, no matter what method or language is used in its production. Furthermore, he observes that because African writers choose not to 'write in African languages does not mean that African languages are going to die.' Quite simply, 'it takes more than just literature to make a language last.'[23] Indeed, the fact that African literature produced in European languages so far has been incredibly effective at communicating the message of resistance against colonial and neo-colonial oppression and cultural imperialism demonstrates the ingenuity of writers who continue to use every available resource to assert their identity.

Support for Achebe's position is also to be found in the work of the important Zimbabwean critic Emmanuel Ngara. Discussing a paper on ethics, ideology and the role of the critic given by Wole Soyinka at a conference on African Literature, Ngara explains:

> Using an African language is not necessarily going to result in the production of better literature. Zimbabwe is an interesting example of a country where the majority of books that have been written are in fact in African languages, and much of the literature that has been written in those languages is of a very inferior quality.[24]

---

[22] Ibid., 61.

[23] Peter W. Vakunta, 'Aporia: Ngugi's Fatalistic Logic of the Unassailable Position of Indigenous Languages in African Literature.' *The Entrepreneur,* May 2, 2010, accessed May 5, 2011, http://www.entrepreneurnewsonline.com/2010/05/aporia-ngugis-fatalistic-logic-of-the-unassailable-position-of-indigenous-languages-in-african-literature.html.

[24] Wole Soyinka, 'Ethics, Ideology and the Critic – From the Discussion,' in *Criticism and Ideology: Second African Writers Conference 1986*, ed. Kirsten Holst Petersen (Uppsala: Scandinavian Institute of African Studies, 1988), 53.

However, right from his first publication, Marechera shows that he is acutely aware of the dilemma of this kind of 'twoness' in all colonized people, especially when it is dramatized by the conflict between one's native language and the colonial language. It is a dilemma that is not easy to resolve since Shona, the mother tongue, the creator of life, is animated by English, the colonial language, the life giver – the route to a good job, a good house, and a good living. Somewhat unsurprisingly, then, the narrator of 'House of Hunger' associates his hallucinations and immobility with the fight between the languages at the back of his mind and soul:

> I began to ramble, incoherently, in a disconnected manner. I was being severed from my own voice. I would listen to it as to a still, small voice coming from the huge distance of the mind. It was like this: English is my second language, Shona my first. When I talked, it was in the form of an interminable argument, one side of which was always expressed in English and the other side always in Shona. At the same time I would be aware of myself as something indistinct but separate from both cultures. I felt gagged by this absurd contest between Shona and English.[25]

In a later story in the same collection of short stories, a friend reads what the narrator writes and finds it 'indigestible.'[26] He asks why the narrator does not write in English? Was it perhaps because he was 'one of those Africans who despised their own roots?'[27] Giving extremely vivid examples from Marechera's oeuvre, George Kahari contends that although Marechera writes in English his images tend to be undeniably Shona.[28] In this way, Marechera can be thought of as exploiting the rich mine of traditional Shona myths, perhaps more so than any other writer of his generation. However, his 'exploitation' of Shona

[25] Dambudzo Marechera, *The House of Hunger* (1978; London: Penguin, 2002), 30.
[26] Dambudzo Marechera, 'Thought-tracks in the Snow,' in *The House of Hunger,* 142-8.
[27] Ibid., 143.
[28] George Kahari, *The Search for Identity and Ufuru: An Introduction to Black Zimbabwean Fiction in English, 1956-1980* (Gweru: Mambo Press, 2009), 273.

mythology is one based on the clever act of compounding and submerging these with myths from other cultures. This, then, explains the genesis of the incipit 'Protista' in the 'Writer's Grain,'[29] which can almost be thought of as a repackaged expression of the very well known Shona folk tale 'Vana vakarasika mugore renzara.'[30] In 'The Servants' Ball,' Marechera demonstrates a deep understanding of typical Shona folk knowledge through the way the servants crack jokes, make music (with the sing-alongs, mbira and guitar), buy each other beer, and criticize one another rather good naturedly.

Be that as it may, 'The Servants' Ball' puts to rest the question of whether Marechera ever wrote in Shona. An artist of Marechera's stature and complexity can never be taken for granted. He was aware, it seems, of his own contradictory nature whenever he opened his mouth or put pen to paper. But, never at any one time did Marechera feel as though he owed anyone an explanation or apology for his writing. In our various disagreements about who he was and why he said or did this and that, we discover that Marechera himself gives us what to talk and disagree about. No wonder he wrote in *The Black Insider* that:

> Everywhere you go, some shit word will collide with you on the wrong side of the road. You can't even hide in yourself because your thoughts think of themselves in the words you have been taught to read and write. Even if you flee home and country, sanity and feeling, the priest and mourners, if any, will be muttering words over your coffin; the people you leave behind will be imagining you in their minds with words and signs. And there will be no silence in the cemetery because always there are burials and more burials of people asphyxiated by words. No wonder it is said,

---

[29] Dambudzo Marechera, 'The Writer's Grain,' in *The House of Hunger,* 100-33.
[30] This and other Shona folk tales can be found in Jane Chifamba's excellent collection. See Jane Chifamba, *Ngano Dzepasichigare* (Oxford: Oxford UP, 1964).

In the beginning was the Word,
And the Word was with God.
And the Word was God,
All things were made by him;
And without him was not any thing made
That was made.[31]

---

[31] Dambudzo Marechera, *The Black Insider*, ed. Flora Veit-Wild (London: Lawrence & Wishart, 1990), 49.

10

Marechera,
the Tree-Poem-Artifact

EDDIE TAY

I am reading Dambudzo Marechera with suspicion, not of him, but of the agenda, conditions and occasions that introduced his writing to me (and to the literary world). I am suspicious of a literary establishment that seeks to contain him within academic criticism. The scholar's proud ownership of the writer may be compared to the colonialist's claim to the land, ignoring the native 'barbarians' and 'savages' who were already there before him and who require civilization and translation. This is Marechera colonized, canonized and collected in print. At the same time, I recognize the limits and irony of my suspicion, acknowledging the very condition of my writing about him. To borrow the words of Max Horkheimer and Theodor W. Adorno from a related context, the triumph of the academic industry is that we feel compelled to use the language of literary criticism even though we see through them.[1] Marechera puts to shame the careerist institutional writer. Marechera in postcolonial literature. Marechera the Zimbabwean poet. Marechera the African author. *Emerging Perspectives on Dambudzo Marechera.* This book. This essay. Is there another way of reading him? Is there a way in which we are able to exit the postcolonialist and/ or academic frame? How may we engage 'the black madman' in an open dance?[2]

I read Marechera close to the text, poet to poet, so as to

---

[1] Max Horkheimer and Theodor W. Adorno, *Dialectic of Enlightenment*, trans. John Cumming (1972; New York: Continuum, 1999), 167.

[2] Dambudzo Marechera, *Cemetery of Mind: Poems by Dambudzo Marechera*, ed. Flora Veit-Wild (Trenton, NJ: Africa World Press, 1992), 7. Unless indicated otherwise, further page references will be given in the main text.

understand his poetic practice. If the coherence of a body of work culminates in its identity, then as we shall see, the Marechera that emerges from the poetry, in terms of his ideological commitment, is as perplexing as the person himself. What gradually emerges from his text is a Marechera that defies a coherent reading. In many ways, this is not surprising – how could someone like Marechera create a coherent body of work? Indeed, how could any poetic practice be coherent and identical to itself? One may even suggest that it is in poetry, a genre that allows for violence to be inflicted upon language to an extent more so than in prose, that we are able to see Marechera in a form that is arguably less mediated by textual conventions. Marechera the poet is more disruptive than Marechera the novelist. Hence, here is another 'emerging perspective:' Marechera the vampire author (more of that later), the drop-out, the non-committal guerilla poet.

Anyone who has ever written creatively would find affinity with Michel de Certeau's notion of textual play described in militant terms, as 'advances and retreats, tactics and games.'[3] In many ways, de Certeau is important for our purposes here, for we have to be mindful of the ways in which a text may be organized, legitimized and interpreted by 'socially authorized professionals and intellectuals.'[4] One must admit there is a certain measure of irony when the work of someone who during his lifetime was wary of being allied with social, political and cultural institutions is now entering mainstream intellectual consciousness. Even as Marechera's work is celebrated by intellectual authorities, we have to be mindful of the fact that Marechera had always been that artless *bricoleur* to authority, adapting materials, voices and styles for his own use. We remind ourselves that for him, it had been an open dance.

[3] Michel de Certeau, *The Practice of Everyday Life*, trans. Steven Rendall (Berkeley: University of California Press, 1984), 175.
[4] Ibid., 171.

I am reading Marechera with suspicion, not of him, but of the agenda, conditions and occasions that introduced his writing to me (and to the literary world). How may one understand him? As his persona proclaims, he has 'nothing to lose but the precious void of self' (24). One may argue that this void of self gestures towards Roland Barthes' assertion that 'writing is the destruction of every voice, of every point of origin.'[5] Are we able to describe him and do justice to his works at one and the same time? We have to learn to read Marechera as a Barthesian scriptor. This is, I believe, the way to restore Marechera to himself. Otherwise, the more we try to describe him and his poetry, the more we are filling the void and hence losing him and his work. Is Marechera to be fused with purpose, agenda, ideology? Dirk Klopper, describing Marechera's work as 'textual madness,' nonetheless calls it a 'productive madness.'[6] While Klopper has given us a very fine and nuanced reading of Marechera's work, I am resisting this impulse to make the writings productive. I read Marechera, not for a pre-given meaning in a text, not to re-constitute his work into a politicized agenda, but to highlight the ways in which Marechera's work frustrates attempts at doing so. As we shall see, many of his poems are acutely reflexive to the extent that they disrupt any attempts at appropriating them for ideological ends. In this way, Marechera's writings free themselves from being pinned down. At the beginning of 'Liberty,' the violence of ideological differences between the two men in the poem is compared to the cataclysmic forces of nature, but by the end of the poem, that force is revealed to be contained, privatized and enclosed within each of the two selves, who are 'now alone / bent on his prey' (3). As readers, we think we are in an open dance, but each of us are, finally, limited to the private universes

---

[5] Roland Barthes, *Image-Music-Text*, trans. Stephen Heath (London: Fontana, 1977), 142.

[6] Dirk Klopper, 'The Outsider Within: Marginality as Symptom in Marechera's "Throne of Bayonets",' in *Emerging Perspectives on Dambudzo Marechera*, eds. Flora Veit-Wild and Anthony Chennells (Trenton, NJ: African World Press, 1999), 124.

of our individual selves. Readers (myself included) may think they are wrestling with their author, but in the final analysis, they are caught up within the private universes of their own readings, pursuing their own prey.

To speak or write about Marechera is to diminish his work. His writing has been sealed by his own hand and locked within his solitude. His writing is silence, a refusal of identity. Anna-Leena Toivanen has rightly argued that in his fiction there is a 'blurring of the boundary between the literary and the extraliterary in Marechera's authorial image.'[7] As we look at his poetry, we discover that it is constantly drawing attention to the limits as well as the potentialities of the text at moments when the self is being represented. While Marechera the person at various times may be described as an iconoclast, outcast, and social misfit, at various moments in his poetry, he opts to be silent to the point of being unnoticeable. In 'The Poems Semantics,' Marechera alludes to Rainer Maria Rilke even as the meaning of his poem exceeds that of Rilke's. Rilke's 'Entrance' is an invitation to a vision, one that liberates the self into the sensory world, allowing for the ineffable to congeal, however tentatively, into signification: 'And as your will seizes on its meaning, / tenderly your eyes let it go.'[8] Rilke's poem is a negotiation between sensory experience and meaning; it establishes a relationship between a clearly delineated subject and object. Marechera's poem, in contrast, sees 'Not the tree / But the poem of the tree' (68). The meta-poem refutes Rilke; it presents not a vision but a reminder that we are constrained within the limits of the text, and furthermore, it is within the space of this text that the persona has been transformed into a tree that he sees (68). It is within this poem-as-artifact that the persona can suddenly become what he sees: 'My arms had

---

[7] Anna-Leena Toivanen, '"At the Receiving End of Severe Misunderstanding:" Dambudzo Marechera's Representations of Authorship,' *Research in African Literatures* 42, no. 1 (2011), 15.

[8] Rainer Maria Rilke, *The Book of Images*, trans. Edward Snow (1902; New York: North Point Press, 1994), 5.

hardened, turned / Into branches' (68). The persona becomes a tree, the subject an object. The poem draws attention to itself as a construct, as an artifact, as a limit as well as a textual space within which anything is possible.

Is it possible to retrieve a politics or an ideological commitment from that tree-poem-artifact that is Marechera? Marechera the poet hides behind the artifact of his poem so as to establish this 'precious void of self' (24). He hides not because he is hiding his message; he hides not because there is a self to hide; he hides because the discourse of poetry demands a self and identity his work cannot offer. This scenario is repeated time and again in his poetry. While the factory hand, milkman, and the soldier are assured of their respective socially productive identities, the persona (let us again call him Marechera) 'like a madman continue[s] to decipher / The print on a shred of blank paper / The print that is to become the poem behind this poem' (99). The problem for Marechera is that his poetry is autogenous. By this, I mean that Marechera's poetic language is a product of its own universe and works apart from society. In Barthes' *Writing Degree Zero*, there is a discussion of how language functions within a poem that best describes Marechera's work:

> The poetic word is here an act without immediate past, without environment, and which holds forth only the dense shadow of reflexes from all sources which are associated with it.[9]

To read Marechera's poetry is to enter into a poetic universe akin to a Platonic world of forms to which our world is made up of shadows on a cave. One is a madman puzzling over Marechera's poetry only because one wishes for it to be 'productive,' to speak, to document, to testify, or to respond to history, politics, ideology and everyday reality.

---

[9] Roland Barthes, *Writing Degree Zero*, trans. Annette Lavers and Colin Smith (New York: Hill and Wang, 1968), 47-8.

Poetic creation for Marechera occurs in the absence of the self, society, agenda, politics, ideology, and even poetic influence. When he invokes other poets, he is not invoking them as his influences, but as encounters out of which there is no affinity. Marechera plunders Rilke's poem so as to emerge with his own. As we have seen earlier in 'Liberty,' for Marechera, to be free is to be alone even as one is wrestling with another. Likewise, in 'To Langston Hughes,' we are offered a fragmentary vision that speaks not of solidarity but difference:

Let me in, Spirit
Nothing out here but darkness
And frantic images
Let me out, body
Nothing in here but darkness
And frantic images (69)

In the poem, both Marechera and Hughes are in the presence of a cosmic wheel on which there are hieroglyphics. It is as if both of them are encountering each other in a cosmological version of the Platonic world of forms, both trying to make sense of the hieroglyphics. Yet there is nothing to be gained from that encounter, and the poem ends with a sense of loss admitting that there is nothing to itself apart from 'darkness / And frantic images.' We are returned time and again to the primal scene of reading and writing. We the readers, together with Marechera, are mad, deciphering poems that do not comment on anything else apart from themselves.

We are confronted with poems shorn of self and agenda, poems that are caught up in self-reflexivity, drawing attention to their own uselessness and lack of signification. Is Marechera a postmodernist then, his work to be compared with the anti-teleological playfulness of Italo Calvino's writings which draw attention to the work as artifact? Marechera is a postmodern poet, not because he embraces postmodernist sensibilities per se. He 'resort[s] to the label / Post-Modernist' because this label is convenient for him and, one may add, for us (43). His poems are always contingent, mobile, elusive, always 'on the go' (25). If pastiche may be regarded as a key postmodern strategy, then Marechera's work is a pastiche of modernist *qua* T.S. Eliot ('The poet's job is to find… the verbal correlative of a particular feeling'), postmodernist, as well as postcolonial sensibilities (209). Hence, the question to ask is not 'whether there is a role at all for postmodernist poetry in the postcolonial state.'[10] To ask that question, to allow the state and the public into Marechera's poetry, is to arrest Marechera's work, hence bringing the sealed privacy of the dance to a close.

It is indeed tempting to locate Marechera's poetry in accordance with identity markers based on ethnicity, nationality, and history and hence violate that private universe of his poetry. It is instructive that Toivanen is aware of the 'problems of instrumentalist approaches' to reading Marechera only to finally admit that as 'some sort of engagement can be considered a necessity in African literatures … that it should be an engagement for a future yet to come.'[11] Toivanen, in a rhetorical move, suspends (or rather, projects) Marechera's political commitment into a utopian 'postcolonial future' so as 'to escape dogmatisms that [she has] distanced [herself] from as a harmful approach to cultural products.'[12] Toivanen's predicament is symptomatic of any attempt at reading Marechera as a postcolonial author. On the one hand, we recognize the close-ended nature of his writings; we recognize his profound skepticism regarding making any sort of pronouncements concerning nation building, colonialism, and ethnicity. On the other hand, his writings exist within a history and society and emerge from a specific social and cultural environment. The result of which is that they lend themselves easily to a postcolonial critique.

In many ways, Marechera's writings can be understood to be

---

[10] Klopper, 'The Outsider Within,' 126.
[11] Toivanen, 'At the Receiving End,' 18.
[12] Ibid., 18.

in a state of tension between being self-enclosed and being a critique of his society. Perhaps Marechera as an author recognizes this dilemma. As he puts it,

> From early in my life I have viewed literature as a unique universe that has no internal divisions. I do not pigeon-hole it by race or language or nation. It is an ideal cosmos co-existing with this crude one.[13]

The above passage indicates that Marechera, too, feels as though his work exists in a self-enclosed state – that it engages with nothing but itself. On the other hand, one page later in his essay, he departs from his earlier statement and poses the following question: 'How can Africa write as if that Black Frenchman, Franz [sic] Fanon, never existed – I refer to the Fanon of *Black Skin, White Mask* [sic].'[14] To invoke Fanon, of course, is to invoke the person we recognize today as a key postcolonial figure.

Marechera overtakes one Fanon but fails to live up to the ideals of another. His poetry exceeds the Fanon of *Black Skin, White Masks* but is found lacking by the standards set by Fanon of *The Wretched of the Earth*. Fanon's *Black Skin, White Masks* is a powerful critique, among many other things, of the way in which the fact of blackness was a fact constructed by the colonizer: 'what is often called a black soul is a white man's artefact.'[15] But Marechera is a *faux* Fanon, inverting Fanon's formulation of the white mask. In 'Fragments,' he mimics and acts out the dance of the postcolonial poet, using and discarding the 'dark silent mask' of his own manufacture, a mask which his poem acknowledges as the facade of 'stubs / of burnt-out stars,' of 'the scrap-iron of a lost empire' (4). The poem is a

---

[13] Dambudzo Marechera, 'The African Writer's Experience of European Literature,' *Zambezia* 14, no. 2 (1987), 99.

[14] Ibid., 100.

[15] Frantz Fanon, *Black Skin, White Masks*, trans. Charles Lam Markmann (New York: Grove Press, 1967), 14.

mask that, when removed, reveals an Eliot-esque landscape of broken images. For Marechera, the black skin is itself a mask. Marechera has no qualms about using that artifact of the dark silent mask to articulate what is essentially a modernist vision of an Africa (or Zimbabwe) in ruins.

His poetry makes a statement that may be appropriated by anyone who wishes to see him as a postcolonial author. However, that very statement is also the limit to which he could be seen as a postcolonial author. He is a postcolonial author with a modernist vision, much as Joseph Conrad's *Heart of Darkness* (1899) possesses a modernist vision of Africa. Yet the modernist conclusion for Marechera is a contingent stance, a temporary stance, a way of making do when no political and/or ideological solutions are tenable. While for Conrad's Marlow, Africa is one of those 'blank spaces on the earth,'[16] for Marechera it is overwritten with the violence of meanings, a place where 'politicians [have] screwed the menace / that curdled the spunk of negritude' (24). Within the Marecherean universe, identity politics is corruption.

Furthermore, the danger in identifying Marechera (or any other author) as a postcolonial author is that the postcolonial is rendered supplementary to nation building discourses and their accompanying social, historical and political formations. It is clear that Marechera's work does not advocate any form of cultural mobilization or identity formation on behalf of a nation. This is why Marechera is unable to provide a satisfactory response to the Fanon of *The Wretched of the Earth*, the book in which Fanon posits an ideal writer that Marechera's writings fail to live up to. It is a revolutionary Fanon who advocates that the writer lives in communion with the people:

> To take part in the African revolution it is not enough to write a revolutionary song; you must fashion the revolution with the

---

[16] Joseph Conrad, *Heart of Darkness* (1899; London: Penguin, 2000), 21.

people. And if you fashion it with the people, the songs will come by themselves, and of themselves.[17]

Marechera's work, in so far as it is associated with social aliena- tion, marginality and disenchantment, is a work that does not live in communion with the people. For him,

> The writer is a vampire, drinking blood – his own blood – a winged creature who flies by night, writing his books. The writer has no duty, no responsibilities, other than to his art. Art is higher than reality.[18]

The notion of the writer as a vampire consuming his own blood is figuratively potent. On the one hand, the vampire figure possesses superhuman abilities; on the other hand, the vampire is dependent on the human for its survival. One may speculate that through the trope of vampirism, Marechera is conveying the vexed condition of being a writer caught between two worlds, between the 'ideal cosmos' and the 'crude' everyday reality.[19] The vampire writer is an autogenous figure. At once transcending and dependent on human reality, the vampire is the undead, just as Marechera is dead as an author (in the Barthesian sense) and alive as a writer belonging to a particular postcolonial milieu. I am reminded here of the final moment in Jorge Luis Borges' 'Borges and I,'[20] where the identity of the narrator/author is presented as singular yet split. We might say the same of Marechera and his work. Marechera is a postcolonial poet as a result of the contingency of reading and writing. His work refuses communion; it rejects community. Likewise, it is of the community. Yet, a postcolonial reading is nevertheless troubling because it is difficult to make Marechera's work correspond to

---

[17] Frantz Fanon, *The Wretched of the Earth*, trans. Constance Farrington (London: Penguin, 1967), 166.

[18] Marechera, 'The African Writer's Experience,' 103.

[19] Ibid., 99.

[20] Jorge Luis Borges, 'Borges and I,' in *Labyrinths: Selected Stories and Other Writings*, Donald A. Yates and James E. Irby (eds), (1962; London: Penguin, 2000), 282-3.

the politicized contents of a society and history and at the same time hold fast to the autogenous nature of his writing.

Marechera, the poet of love, presents a different kind of 'problem.' The problem with love poetry for any poet is that it expresses a universal and hence unoriginal impulse. To be understood, in this case, is to be unoriginal. There is at first glance no ideological profit to be extracted from love poetry. However, love in its heterosexual form is not just an affect but an institutionalizing force. It bears the seed of domesticity and familial order. It is a socialization impulse, an organizing principle, a foundation upon which rests a community, nation, and state. It is, as Marechera himself puts it, 'centripetal' (215). Love is meaning and hence, teleology. This, one may speculate, is why love poetry becomes a fecund ground for Marechera's writing.

Marechera's Amelia poems represent the very antithesis of meaning. In his hands, love poetry (and love) becomes a dissembling force. For Marechera, love poetry and its attendant impulses are no longer possible and for him, to write of love is to present a facade *as* a facade. It is to write of

One who behind polite phrases
Screamed terrible curses to the sky;
One whose slow measured pace to the altar
Raised more dust than buffalo stampeding (169)

The reflexivity that is characteristic of Marechera is no less present in these sonnets. To write love poetry is to focus on the interiority of the self, to the extent that even literary allusions are repulsive forces:

But my Dark Lady a delightful phantom to dethrone
Daughter of dung (fecund development)
I just can't dig her shit all the time. (184)

Certainly, we are meant to recognize the references to Shakespeare's sonnets. Many of Shakespeare's sonnets, even as they playfully subvert the courtly norms evoked by the poetic form, are nevertheless witty, elegant and intelligent. In contrast, Marechera's sonnets are irreverent to the point of being crude. Commentators such as Stewart Crehan have written of Marechera's 'Rabelaisian braggadocio' pertaining to his attitude toward African nation building.[21] Yet this carnivalesque tendency is found no less in the Amelia sonnets. Love, it seems, receives the same treatment in Marechera's work as political ideology.

What this implies is that there is an anarchist tendency, by which I mean not a political philosophy advocating a stateless society but that the individual, idiosyncratic, and the interiority of the self becomes a force that overrides and overrules love poetry (and by extension, poetry or literature itself) as a socializing and organizing impulse. Amelia is a function of the autogenous nature of Marechera's poetics and hence not available for public scrutiny, 'All that's left of Amelia is all this pottery / Silent, soothing, yet eerily arranged around my memories' (171). Instead of seeking to facilitate comprehension, time and again, as in the above lines, the reader is placed at the exterior of the writing and of the self. Amelia exists, but as fragments and residual poetic elements that has yet to be formed. Even the persona assumes a ghostly aspect, 'As I rise from lust's foul roadside and parkbench / I see in the hideous darkness before me her serene eyes glowing softly' (171). The insularity and narcissism of the poem, in a self-conscious manner, places the reader on the outside. 'I' becomes the centre of the poem, and it is the persona, not the reader, who sees Amelia. At various moments, Marechera avoids the imagistic possibilities of the poem and uses instead opaque phrases ('eerily arranged,' 'hideous darkness'), hence drawing attention to the failure of his poem which, as an act of recollection, is according to him 'too blunt an instrument' for the reader (171). This 'I,' a haunting specter found at roadsides

---

[21] Stewart Crehan, 'Down and Out in London and Harare: Marechera's Subversion of "African Literature",' in *Emerging Perspectives on Dambudzo Marechera*, 269.

and park benches, exists on the same plane with his beloved; it elects to alienate itself from his readers, from concrete reality, and from society.

Thus Amelia becomes that signifier in a relay consisting of the self, desire, demon, memory, fragment of a nightmare, poem: Amelia is 'what I was' (174); she is 'the ghost of my youth's bitter longings' (174); she has 'horns and forked tail' (174); she is a 'recollection' (171); she was 'unfaithful in heaven' in a dream (172); and she possesses 'stanza-lips' (169). The Amelia poems are caught within their own imaginary textual circuit, the subject moving from one thing to another under another name, unable to signify anything apart from itself. The poems are self-consuming (not unlike a vampire drinking his own blood). This lack of signification of anything apart from itself, I propose, is the form of madness of which Marechera writes in his poems. Here, I am reminded of Foucault and of what he has written concerning madness:

> Madness appears as an utterance wrapped up in itself, articulating something else beneath what it says, of which it is at the same time the only possible code – an esoteric language, if you will, since it confines its linguistic code within an utterance that ultimately does not articulate anything other than this implication.[22]

Foucault's 'Madness, the Absence of Work' opens with the hope that madness in the future might 'constitute the indispensable grids through which we and our culture become legible.'[23] For now, Marechera's poetry is that esoteric code we have yet to read. His language is a border protecting a wellspring of meaning inherent in his writing. We have to accept the madness of Marechera's writing, a self-consuming madness that is explicitly stated and enacted in so many of his poems.

We cannot read Marechera properly. Or, to put it in another

---

[22] Michel Foucault, 'Madness, the Absence of Work,' *Critical Inquiry* 21, no. 2 (1995), 295.
[23] Ibid., 290.

way, we can read Marechera properly only if we fully deny the text its *unproductive* madness. I believe that this proper way of reading Marechera is incorrect. If we are able to co-opt Marechera's work to do the work of postcolonialism, it is because we are trying to render the madness productive. But because we cannot fully erase the marks of madness from his writings, Marechera then becomes that postcolonial writer who is writing from a place of marginality in relation to those in power. Marechera then is a postcolonial author insofar as he is read as a victim of dominant social, cultural and political forces. We are able to speak of a 'postmodern,' 'modernist,' or a 'carnivalesque' Marechera, but these are poses the madman assumes as contingencies. Marechera's poetry is not a medium through which he explores issues, topics, themes, not a depository of his frustrations, not a location of his historical self that one finds so vexing. Rather, it is a form he wrestles with ('Will this moon scrap itself off my poems!'), a form with a literary history he is engaging in a combative manner, hoping to find a space 'between English school / And [his] cockroach voice' (99). We have to repress the textual madness and his 'cockroach voice' if we wish to read him properly. This, of course, is unacceptable if one accepts that madness lies at the heart of his writing.

Adorno has written, 'In the end, the writer is not even allowed to live in his writing' and this I believe applies to Marechera's posthumous fate.[24] I argue that there is a need for us to retain our lack of understanding of Marechera. Again, to quote Foucault: 'madness has appeared not like the ruse of a hidden signification but like a prodigious *reserve* of meaning.'[25] It is this reserve within his poetry that we have to protect, instead of rendering them 'productive' for the formation of discourse, for theory, for politics. In the seminal *Dambudzo Marechera: A*

---

[24] Theodor Adorno, *Minima Moralia: Reflections from Damaged Life*, trans. E.F.N. Jephcott (London: Verso, 1974), 87.
[25] Foucault, 'Madness, the Absence of Work,' 295.

Source Book on his Life and Work, Flora Veit-Wild has written of how Marechera is now a cult figure amongst a new generation of readers who regard him as 'the hero of the poor peasants and the proletariat.'[26] While I do not deny the positive political potential of reading Marechera's work in this manner, I am proposing that we have to learn to be silent in front of the tree-poem-artifact that is Marechera, who has read his own poetry in such a way that he believed his work would be disavowed: 'I am the luggage no one will claim' (199). I read this line not as a prophecy but as the desire of the text to be left alone, to be unused, unproductive and unclaimed. In other words, we have to learn how to stop reading productively so as to preserve the various other possibilities of his poetry, possibilities we have yet to learn to read. Even as we acknowledge that his writing is compelling, we have to stop short of our readings and accept that the meaning of his work will never quite fully arrive. We have to be silent so that his poetry may one day be adequate to the promise of these lines he has written:

> Out of the blue egg
> A ruffled pulsing yellow hatches (120)

[26] Flora Veit-Wild, *Dambudzo Marechera: A Source Book on his Life and Work* (London: Hans Zell, 1992), 382.

Bibliography

Achebe, Chinua. *Morning Yet on Creation Day*. London: Heinemann, 1975.

Adorno, Theodor. *Minima Moralia: Reflections from Damaged Life*. Translated by E.F.N. Jephcott. London: Verso, 1974.

Aldiss, Brian W., and David Wingrove. *Trillion Year Spree: The History of Science Fiction*. London: Victor Gollancz, 1986.

Althusser, Louis. *Lenin and Philosophy and Other Essays*. Translated by Ben Brewster. London: Monthly Review Press, 1971.

Ashcroft, Bill, Gareth Griffiths and Helen Tiffin. *The Empire Writes Back: Theory and Practice in Post-colonial Literatures*. London: Routledge, 1989.

Bakhtin, Mikhail. *The Dialogic Imagination*. Edited by Michael Holquist. Translated by Caryl Emerson and Michael Holquist. Austin: University of Texas Press, 1981.

Bakhtin, Mikhail. *Rabelais and His World*. Translated by Hélène Iswolsky. Bloomington: Indiana UP, 1984.

Bakunin, Mikhail, 'The Paris Commune and the Idea of the State' (1871). In *Writings on the Paris Commune: Marx, Engels, Bakunin, Kropotkin, and Lenin*, 75-88. St Petersburg, FL: Red and Black Publishers, 2008.

Barthes, Roland. *Writing Degree Zero*. Translated by Annette Lavers and Colin Smith. New York: Hill and Wang, 1968.

Barthes, Roland. *S/Z: An Essay*. Translated by Richard Miller. New York: Hill and Wang, 1974.

Barthes, Roland. *Image-Music-Text*. Translated by Stephen Heath. London: Fontana, 1977.

Benjamin, Walter. 'Theses on the Philosophy of History' (1940). In *Illuminations: Essays and Reflections*, translated by Harry Zorn, 245-55. London: Pimlico, 1999.

Bernasconi, Robert. 'The Assumption of Negritude: Aimé Césaire, Frantz Fanon, and the Vicious Circle of Racial Politics.' *Parallax* 8, no. 2 (2002): 69–83.

Bhabha, Homi K. *The Location of Culture*. London: Routledge, 1994.

Bloom, Clive. *Literature, Politics and Intellectual Crisis in Britain Today*. Basingstoke: Palgrave Macmillan, 2001.

Boehmer, Elleke. *Stories of Women: Gender and Narrative in the Postcolonial Nation*. Manchester: Manchester UP, 2005.

Bookchin, Murray. *Post-Scarcity Anarchism*. Berkeley: Ramparts Press, 1971.

Borges, Jorge Luis. 'Borges and I.' In *Labyrinths: Selected Stories and Other Writings*, edited by Donald A. Yates and James E. Irby, 282-3. 1962; London: Penguin, 2000.

Bryce, Jane. 'Inside/out: Body and Sexuality in Dambudzo Marechera's Fiction.' In *Emerging Perspectives on Dambudzo Marechera*, edited by Flora Veit-Wild and Anthony Chennells, 221-34. Trenton, NJ: Africa World Press, 1999.

Buuck, David. 'African Doppelganger: Hybridity and Identity in the Work of Dambudzo Marechera.' *Research in African Literatures* 28, no. 2 (Summer 1997): 118-31.

Call, Lewis. *Postmodern Anarchism*. Boston: Lexington Books, 2002.

Camus, Albert. *The Rebel*. Translated by Anthony Bower. 1951; London: Penguin, 2000.

Chifamba, Jane. *Ngano Dzepasichigare*. Oxford: Oxford UP, 1964.

Chinweizu, Onwuchekwa Jemie, and Ihechukwu Madubuike. *Towards the Decolonization of African Literature*. London: Taylor & Francis, 1985.

Chiwome, Emmanuel. *A Social History of the Shona Novel*. Kadoma: Juta, 1996.

Clark, Katerina and Michael Holquist. *Mikhail Bakhtin*. Cambridge, Mass.: Harvard UP, 1984.

Comte, Auguste, *The Essential Comte*. Edited by Stanislav Andreski. New York: Harper and Row, 1974.

Conrad, Joseph. *Heart of Darkness*. 1899; London: Penguin, 2000.

Cooper, David. *The Death of the Family*. Middlesex: Penguin Books, 1971.

Crehan, Stewart. 'Review of Flora Veit-Wild *Dambudzo Marechera: A Source Book on his Life and Work*.' *Research in African Literatures* 25, no. 2 (Summer 1994): 197-200.

Crehan, Stewart. 'Down and Out in London and Harare: Marechera's Subversion of "African Literature".' In *Emerging Perspectives on Dambudzo Marechera*, edited by Flora Veit-Wild and Anthony Chennells, 265-281. Trenton, NJ: Africa World Press, 1999.

Debord, Guy. *The Society of The Spectacle*. Translated by Donald Nicholson Smith. New York: Zone Books, 1995.

de Certeau, Michel. *The Practice of Everyday Life*. Translated by Steven Rendall. Berkeley: University of California Press, 1984.

Deleuze, Gilles. *Nietzsche and Philosophy*. Translated by Hugh Tomlinson. London: Athlone Press, 1983.

Deleuze, Gilles. *Negotiations, 1972–1990*. Translated by Martin Joughin. New York: Columbia UP, 1995.

Deleuze, Gilles. *Essays Critical and Clinical*. Translated by Daniel W. Smith and Michael Greco. London: Verso, 1998.

Deleuze, Gilles and Félix Guattari. *A Thousand Plateaus: Capitalism and Schizophrenia 2*. Translated by Brian Massumi. London: Athlone, 1988.

Derrida, Jacques. *Speech and Phenomena: And Other Essays on Husserl's Theory of Signs*. Translated by David B. Allison. Evanston, IL: Northwestern University Press, 1973.

Derrida, Jacques. *Of Grammatology*. Translated by Gayatri Chakravorty Spivak. Baltimore: The Johns Hopkins UP, 1974.

Derrida, Jacques. 'The Law of Genre.' *Critical Inquiry* 7.1 (Autumn 1980): 55-81.

Derrida, Jacques. *The Other Heading: Reflections on Today's Europe*. Translated by Pascale-Anne Brault and Michael B. Naas. Bloomington: Indiana UP, 1992.

Esslin, Martin. *The Theatre of the Absurd*. London: Eyre and Spottiswoode, 1962.

Esty, Joshua, D. 'Excremental Postcolonialism.' *Contemporary Literature* 41, no. 1 (1999): 22–59.

Evenson, Brian. 'Zimbabwe's Beat Generation.' In *Thus Spake the Corpse: An Exquisite Corpse Reader 1988-1998 vol. 2*, edited by Andrei Codrescu and Laura Rosenthal, 357-9. Santa Rosa, CA: Black Sparrow Press, 1999.

Eze, Chielo Zona. *The Trial of Robert Mugabe*. Chicago: Okri Books, 2009.

Fanon, Frantz. *The Wretched of the Earth*. Translated by Constance Farrington. New York: Grove Press, 1961.

Fanon, Frantz. *Black Skin, White Masks*. Translated by Charles Lam Markmann. New York: Grove Press, 1967; London: Pluto Press, 1986.

Foucault, Michel. 'Madness, the Absence of Work.' *Critical Inquiry* 21, no. 2 (1995): 290-298.

Forth, Christopher. 'Intellectual Anarchy and Imaginary Otherness: Gender, Class, and Pathology in French Intellectual Discourse, 1890-1900.' *The Sociological Quarterly* 37, no. 4 (Autumn, 2006): 645-71.

Gagiano, Annie. *Achebe, Head, Marechera: On Power and Change in Africa*. Boulder, CO:

Lynne Rienner, 2000.

Gagiano, Annie. 'Marecheran Postmodernism: Mocking the Bad Joke of "African Modernity".' *Journal of Literary Studies* 18, no. 1 (2002): 61-84.

Gaylard, Gerald. *After Colonialism: African Postmodernism and Magical Realism.* Johannesburg: Witwatersrand UP, 2006.

Godwin, William. *Enquiry Concerning Political Justice: with selections from Godwin's other writings.* Oxford: Clarendon Press, 1971.

Gordon, Jean. 'Reveling in Genre: An Interview with China Miéville.' *Science Fiction Studies* 30.3 (November 2003): 355-73.

Greenland, Colin. *The Entropy Exhibition: Michael Moorcock and the UK 'New Wave.'* London: Routledge & Kegan Paul, 1983.

Habila, Helon. 'On Dambudzo Marechera: The Life and Times of an African Writer.' *The Virginian Quarterly Review* (Winter, 2006): 251-60.

Hallward, Peter. *Absolutely Postcolonial: Writing Between the Singular and the Specific.* Manchester: Manchester UP, 2001.

Hardt, Michael, and Antonio Negri. *Empire.* Cambridge, MA: Harvard UP, 2000.

Harvey, Irene E. *Labyrinths of Exemplarity: At the Limits of Deconstruction.* Albany: State University of New York Press, 2002.

Horkheimer, Max and Theodor W. Adorno. *Dialectic of Enlightenment.* Translated by John Cumming. 1972; New York: Continuum, 1999.

Huddart, David. *Postcolonial Theory and Autobiography.* London: Routledge, 2008.

Ibrahim, Huma. 'The Violated Universe: Neo-Colonial Sexual and Political Consciousness in Dambudzo Marechera.' *Research in African Literatures* 21, no. 2 (1990): 79–90.

James, Darius. *Negrophobia: An Urban Parable.* New York: Citadel, 1992.

Joyce, James. *Ulysses: The 1922 Text.* 1922; Oxford: Oxford UP, 2008.

Kahari, George. *The Search for Identity and Ufuru.* Gweru: Mambo Press, 2009.

Kaulemu, David. 'The Culture of Party Politics and the Concept of the State.' In *Zimbabwe: The Past is the Future*, edited by David Harold-Barry, 77-86. Harare: Weaver, 2004.

Klopper, Dirk. 'The Outsider Within: Marginality as Symptom in Marechera's "Throne of Bayonets".' In *Emerging Perspectives on Dambudzo Marechera*, edited by Flora Veit-Wild and Anthony Chennells, 121-35. Trenton, NJ: Africa World Press, 1999.

Kristeva, Julia. *Powers of Horror: An Essay on Abjection.* Translated by Leon S. Roudiez. New York: Columbia UP, 1982.

Lansu, Alle. 'Escape from the "House of Hunger:" Marechera Talks about His Life.' In *Dambudzo Marechera: A Source Book on his Life and Work*, by Flora Veit-Wild, 1-48. London: Hans Zell, 1992.

Levin, Melissa and Laurice Taitz. 'Fictional Autobiographies or Autobiographical Fictions?' In *Emerging Perspectives on Dambudzo Marechera*, edited by Flora Veit-Wild and Anthony Chennells, 163-76. Trenton, NJ: Africa World Press, 1999.

Lilford, Grant. 'Traces of Tradition: The Probability of the Marecheran Manfish.' In *Emerging Perspectives on Dambudzo Marechera*, edited by Flora Veit-Wild and Anthony Chennells, 283-98. Trenton, NJ: Africa World Press, 1999.

Lopes, Henri. 'My Novels, My Characters, and Myself.' *Research in African Literatures* 24, no. 1 (Spring 1993): 81-6.

Marechera, Dambudzo. *The House of Hunger.* London: Heinemann, 1978; London: Penguin, 2002.

Marechera, Dambudzo. *Black Sunlight.* London: Heinemann, 1980.

Marechera, Dambudzo. *Mindblast, or, The Definitive Buddy.* Harare: College Press, 1984.

Marechera, Dambudzo. 'Soyinka, Dostoevsky: the Writer on Trial for his Time.' *Zambezia* 14, no. 2 (1987): 106-12.

Marechera, Dambudzo. 'The African Writer's Experience of European Literature.' *Zambezia* 14, no. 2 (1987): 99-111.

Marechera, Dambudzo. *Cemetery of Mind*. Edited by Flora Veit-Wild. Trenton, NJ: Africa World Press, 1992.

Marechera, Dambudzo. *The Black Insider*. Edited by Flora Veit-Wild. Trenton, NJ: Africa World Press, 1992; Harare: Baobab Books, 1990; London: Laurence and Wishart.1990.

Marechera, Dambudzo. *Scrapiron Blues*. Edited by Flora Veit-Wild. Harare: Baobab Books, 1994.

Marshall, Peter. *Demanding the Impossible: A History of Anarchism*. London: Fontana, 1993.

Matthews, J.H. *The Surrealist Mind*. London: Associated UP, 1991.

Mbembe, Achille. *On the Postcolony*. Translated by A. M. Berrett, Janet Roitman, Murray Last, and Steven Rendall. Berkeley: University of California Press, 2001.

Mehlman, Jeffrey and Brian Massumi. Editors and Translators. *Foucault/Blanchot: Maurice Blanchot: The Thought from Outside and Michel Foucault as I Imagine Him*. New York: Zone Books, 1987.

Mendlesohn, Farah. *Rhetorics of Fantasy*. Middletown, CT: Wesleyan UP, 2008.

Miéville, China. *Perdido Street Station*. London: Macmillan, 2000.

Miéville, China. *The Scar*. London: Macmillan, 2002.

Mlambo, Obert. 'Resurrecting the Teaching of Classics in Zimbabwe's Secondary Schools: The Imperative for a New Paradigm in Zimbabwe's Education Approach.' *Zimbabwe Journal of Educational Research* 23, no. 1 (2011): 50-63.

Moore-Gilbert, Bart. *Postcolonial Life-Writing: Culture, Politics and Self-Representation*. London: Routledge, 2009.

Morris, Pam, ed. *The Bakhtin Reader: Selected Writings of Bakhtin, Medvedev, Voloshinov*. London: Edward Arnold, 1984.

Mtisi, Joseph, Munyaradzi Nyakudya, and Teresa Barnes. 'War in Rhodesia, 1965-1980.' In *Becoming Zimbabwe*, edited by Brian Raftopolous and Alois Mlambo, 141-66. Weaver Press: Harare, 2009.

Ngara, Emmanuel. *Art and Ideology in the African Novel: A Study of the Influence of Marxism on the African Novel*. Oxford: Heinemann, 1985.

Ngara, Emmanuel and Fay Chung. *Socialism, Education and Development: A Challenge to Zimbabwe*. Harare: Zimbabwe Publishing House, 1985.

Ngugi wa Thiong'o. *Decolonising the Mind: The Politics of Language in African Literature*. Harare: Zimbabwe Publishing House; London: James Currey, 1981.

Nyarota, Geof. 'Willowgate Revisited Two Decades Later.' *The Standard*, April 16, 2006. Accessed May 5, 2011. http://www.thestandard.co.zw/?view=article&id=15274.

Okonkwo, Juliet. 'A Review of *The House of Hunger*.' *Okike: An African Journal of New Writing* (June 1981): 87-91.

Parpart, Jane L. 'Masculinities, Race and Violence in the Making of Zimbabwe.' In *Manning the Nation: Father Figures in Zimbabwean Literature and Society*, edited by Kizito Z. Muchemwa and Robert Muponde, 102-14. Harare: Weaver, 2007.

Parker, Kenneth. 'Home is Where the Heart ... Lies.' *Transition* 59 (1993): 65-77.

Pattison, David. 'Call No Man Happy: Inside *The Black Insider*, Marechera's Journey to Become a Writer?' *Journal of Southern African Studies* 20, no. 2 (June 1994): 221-39.

Perez, Rolando. *An(archy) and Schizoanalysis*. New York: Automedia, 1990.

Perocchio, Patrizia. 'A Black Insider: The Man Walking Away From His Shadow.' In *Emerging Perspectives on Dambudzo Marechera*, edited by Flora Veit-Wild and Anthony Chennells, 209-20. Trenton, NJ: Africa World Press, 1999.

Petersen, Kirsten Holst. *An Articulate Anger: Dambudzo Marechera, 1952–87*. Sydney: Dangaroo Press, 1988.

Proudhon, Pierre-Joseph. *What is Property?* (1840) Edited by Donald R. Kelley and Bonnie G. Smith. Cambridge: Cambridge UP, 1994.

Proudhon, Pierre-Joseph. *The General Idea of the Revolution in the Nineteenth Century.* 1851; New York: Cosimo, 2007.

Raftopoulos, Brian. 'Beyond the House of Hunger: Democratic Struggle in Zimbabwe.' *Review of African Political Economy* 20, no. 55 (November 1992): 57-66.

Reiman, Donald and Neil Fraistat. *Shelley's Poetry and Prose: Authoritative Texts and Criticism.* New York: WW Norton & Co, 2002.

Richardson, Michael, and Krzystof Fijalkowski, eds, *Surrealism Against the Current.* London: Pluto Press, 2001.

Rilke, Rainer Maria. *The Book of Images.* Translated by Edward Snow. 1902; New York: North Point Press, 1994.

Roberts, Adam. *The History of Science Fiction.* Basingstoke: Palgrave Macmillan, 2007.

Russo, Mary. *The Female Grotesque: Risk, Excess and Modernity.* New York: Routledge, 1994.

Said, Edward. 'The Mind of Winter: Reflections on Life in Exile.' *Harper's Magazine,* September, 1984.

Said, Edward. *Culture and Imperialism.* London: Chatto & Windus, 1992.

Seda, Owen S. 'The Fourth Dimension: Dambudzo Marechera as a Dramatist – An Analysis of Two Plays.' In *Zimbabwean Transitions: Essays on Zimbabwean Literature in English, Ndebele and Shona,* edited by Mbongeni Z. Malaba and Geoffrey V. Davis, 147-58. Amsterdam: Rodopi, 2007.

Selden, Daniel. 'Genre of Genre.' In *The Search for the Ancient Novel,* edited by James Tatum, 39-64. Baltimore: John Hopkins UP, 1994.

Shadur Mark. 'Labour Relations in Zimbabwean Parastatal.' *Zambezia* 18, no. 1 (1991): 25-34.

Shaw, Drew. 'Transgressing Traditional Narrative Form.' In *Emerging Perspectives on Dambudzo Marechera,* edited by Flora Veit-Wild and Anthony Chennells, 3-22. Trenton, NJ: Africa World Press, 1999.

Shelley, Percy Bysshe. *The Masque of Anarchy.* London: Edward Moxon, 1832.

Shelley, Percy Bysshe. *A Defence of Poetry and Other Essays.* Gloucester: Dodo Press, 2007.

Sibanda, Eliakim. *The Zimbabwe African People's Union 1961–87: A Political History of Insurgency in Southern Rhodesia.* Trenton, NJ: Africa World Press, 2005.

Slemon, Stephen. 'Magic Realism as Postcolonial Discourse.' In *Magic Realism: Theory, History, Community,* edited by Lois Parkinson Zamora and Wendy B. Faris, 407-26. Durham: Duke UP, 1995.

Smith, Robert. *Derrida and Autobiography.* Cambridge: Cambridge UP, 1995.

Smith, Sidonie and Julia Watson. 'The Trouble with Autobiography: Cautionary Notes for Narrative Theorists.' In *A Companion to Narrative Theory,* edited by James Phelan and Peter Rabinowitz, 356-71. Oxford: Blackwell, 2005.

Soyinka, Wole. 'Ethics, Ideology and the Critic – From the Discussion.' In *Criticism and Ideology: Second African Writers Conference 1986,* edited by Kirsten Holst Petersen, 51-4. Uppsala: Scandinavian Institute of African Studies, 1988.

Tatum, James, ed. *The Search for the Ancient Novel.* Baltimore: John Hopkins UP, 1994.

Thomas, Lorenzo. 'Alea's Children: The Avant-Garde on the Lower East Side, 1960-1970.' *African American Review* 27, no. 4 (Winter, 1993): 573-8.

Todorov, Tzvetan. *Mikhail Bakhtin: The Dialogical Principle.* Translated by Wlad Godzich. Minneapolis: University of Minneapolis Press, 1984.

Toivanen, Anna-Leena. '"At the Receiving End of Severe Misunderstanding:" Dambudzo Marechera's Representations of Authorship.' *Research in African Literatures* 42, no. 1 (2011): 14-31.

Vakunta, Peter W. 'Aporia: Ngugi's Fatalistic Logic of the Unassailable Position of Indigenous Languages in African Literature.' *The Entrepreneur*, May 2, 2010. Accessed May 5, 2011. http://www.entrepreneurnewsonline.com/2010/05/aporia-ngugis-fatalistic-logic-of-the-unassailable-position-of-indigenous-languages-in-african-literature.html.

Vambe, Maurice Taonezvi. *African Oral Story-telling Tradition and the Zimbabwean Novel in English*. Pretoria: UNISA Press, 2004.

Vambe, Maurice Taonezvi. 'Orality in the Black Zimbabwean Novel in English.' *Journal of Southern African Studies* 30, no. 2 (June 2004): 235-249.

VanderMeer, Jeff and Ann VanderMeer, eds, *The New Weird*. San Francisco: Tachyon, 2008.

Veit-Wild, Flora. 'Words as Bullets: The Writings of Dambudzo Marechera.' *Zambezia* 14, no. 2 (1987): 113-20.

Veit-Wild, Flora. *Patterns of Poetry in Zimbabwe*. Gweru: Mambo Press, 1988.

Veit-Wild, Flora. *Dambudzo Marechera: A Source Book on his Life and Work*. London: Hans Zell, 1992.

Veit-Wild, Flora. 'Carnival and Hybridity in Texts by Dambudzo Marechera and Lesego Rampolokeng.' *Journal of Southern African Studies* 23, no. 4 (December, 1997): 553-64.

Veit-Wild, Flora. *Writing Madness: Borderlines of the Body in African Literature*. Harare: Weaver Press; Oxford: James Currey, 2006.

Veit-Wild, Flora and Ernst Schade, eds, *Dambudzo Marechera, 1952-1987*. Harare: Baobab Books, 1988.

Veit-Wild, Flora and Anthony Chennells, eds, *Emerging Perspectives on Dambudzo Marechera*. Trenton, NJ: Africa World Press, 1999.

Vergès, Françoise. 'To Cure and to Free.' In *Fanon: A Critical Reader*, edited by Lewis R. Gordon, T. Denean Sharpley-Whiting and Renée T. White, 85-99. Oxford: Blackwell, 1996.

Vergès, Françoise. 'Creole Skin, Black Mask: Fanon and Disavowal.' *Critical Inquiry* 23, no. 3 (Spring 1997): 578–95.

Volk, Daniela. '"In Search of my True People:" Universal Humanism in Marechera's Writing.' In *Emerging Perspectives on Dambudzo Marechera*, edited by Flora Veit-Wild and Anthony Chennells, 299-314. Trenton, NJ: Africa World Press, 1999.

Wali, Obiajunwa. 'The Dead End of African Literature?' *Transition* 10 (September 1963): 13-16.

Zeleza, Paul Tiyambe. 'The Democratic Transition in Africa and the Anglophone Writer.' *Canadian Journal of African Studies/Revue Canadienne des Études Africaines* 28, no. 3 (1994): 472-97.

Zeleza, Paul Tiyambe. 'The Politics and Poetics of Exile: Edward Said in Africa.' *Research in African Literatures* 36, no. 3 (Autumn 2005): 1-22.

Zhuwarara, Rino. *Introduction to Zimbabwean Literature*. Harare: College Press, 2001.

Zimunya, Musaemura. *Those Years of Drought and Hunger: The Birth of Black Zimbabwean Literature in English*. Gweru: Mambo Press, 1982.

Zinyemba, Ranga. 'Zimbabwe's "Lost" Novelists in Search of Direction.' *Moto* 15, no. 7 (August 1983): 9-10.

Index